More praise for 'Leadership Unplugged' by Jacqueline Moore and Steven Sonsino

'In *Leadership Unplugged*, Jacqueline Moore and Steven Sonsino have dedicated themselves to exploring how and why conversations are a foundation of great leadership. They zero in on leadership communications through two-way communications and their direct impact on organizational strategy. They emphasise the importance of uncomfortable conversations and offer readers a thoughtful framework linking debate, discussions and dialogue together so that managers can understand the complete lifecycle of leadership communications.'

— *Jay A. Conger, Professor of Organizational Behaviour, London Business School*

'In *Leadership Unplugged*, Jacqueline Moore and Steven Sonsino have defined an innovative way of leading that is breathtakingly simple. From their detailed knowledge of the way communication works at every level – between people and between organizations – they have analysed for us and defined ways of communicating that every executive around the world can benefit from.'

— *Kay Grenz, Vice President for Human Resources, 3M, St Paul*

'Learned yet practical.'

— *Harvard Business Press Online*

THE SEVEN FAILINGS OF REALLY USELESS LEADERS

First published 2007 by
MSL Publishing
29 Harley Street, London W1G 9QR

ISBN 978-1-905587-00-1 case bound

A catalogue record for this book is available from the British Library.

A catalog record for this book is available from the Library of Congress.

Printed and bound in England by
Cambridge University Press

THE SEVEN FAILINGS OF REALLY USELESS LEADERS

How to Inspire Your People to Higher Levels of Performance, Productivity and Profitability

Jacqueline Moore
& Steven Sonsino

MSL PUBLISHING

LONDON

This book is dedicated to the unsung senior, junior and middle managers we work with on a daily basis. Without your frustrations, your insights and your experience, this book would not have been written.

You challenged us to make leadership skills practical and tangible. If we've been successful in this, we challenge you now to have the courage to lead in a different, more authentic way.

ACKNOWLEDGEMENTS

WRITING A BOOK MAY appear to be a solitary endeavour, but the reality is that if you want a book to be read by thousands or hopefully tens of thousands of people, you need to have an entire team on your side.

At the head of the queue we have to thank our children, Christopher, Amelia and Michael, who had to suffer our long absences overseas or our long absences chained to the keyboard during the creation of this book. We love you dearly and hope you'll never need this book.

Next a huge thank you to our colleagues at London Business School, the European School of Management and Technology in Berlin and Escola Gestão do Porto in Portugal. Without your commitment and comradeship many of these ideas would never have seen the light of day. Thank you for allowing us to test these ideas in executive education programmes, lectures and seminars.

Thanks to Kim Grace for the cover photography and for some great conversations at odd times of the day, and thanks also to Tanja Kappler for her advice and help with the cover.

A big thank you to Cambridge University Press who saw us through the minefield of publishing to an incredibly tight schedule. Special thanks there to Duncan Roeser, Tony Mansfield and Lorraine Lee. Transatlantic thanks also to Randy Gilbert and Peggy McColl who helped us launch the book.

Finally we are deeply grateful to all of our seminar attendees, support staff and joint venture partners. Without you there would be no life-changing seminars.

CONTENTS

THE FOUR
PERSONAL FAILINGS

THE EIGHTH FAILING

APPENDICES

FIGURES

Inspire your people and boost the bottom line

What can you learn from the
Seven Failings of Really Useless Leaders?

PEOPLE ARE SHOCKED AT the beginning of our work-shops when one of the first things we say to them is not to believe a word we say. 'You've got to make your own mind up,' we suggest. Why would we say that? Well, it's because we can only speak from our own experience. None of the concepts or insights we'll share with you – either here in this book or on our leadership seminars – is inherently true or false, right or wrong. They simply reflect our own opinions, the research we've conducted, the scholarly studies we've reviewed and the results we've seen in the lives of hundreds if not thousands of managers

Of course, many of the executives who come to our work-shops and seminars come to us explicitly for 'The Answer', hoping for a quick fix to their most challenging management problems: how to inspire their people to higher levels of performance, productivity and profitability. Unfortunately no one – to our knowledge – has the single undisputed answer to this challenge. We do believe, though, that if you use the simple principles outlined in *The Seven Failings of Really Useless Leaders* you can transform your leadership style. You can become an even more inspirational leader than you already are. But don't just read this book. Study it as if your life depended on it. (Your business life, at least.) Then try the principles out for yourself. Practise. Then, whatever works you just keep on doing. Whatever doesn't work you're welcome to throw away.

At this point some readers may be wondering whether we're able to help them at all. If you've found yourself asking the same thing, don't worry, you're not alone. Perhaps a story that Steven tells can shed some light.

'A tall, bookish man with little round spectacles sidled up to me during the Wednesday morning coffee break. We were halfway through a week-long leadership workshop at London Business School and I could see him slowly making his way over. He introduced himself and we chatted for a while. And then he asked me the question. "So tell me," he said, half joking, but half in deadly earnest, "what do I have to do to become an inspirational leader?"

'I paused, looking straight at him over the top of my coffee cup. "I'm beginning to think that's the wrong question," I said. "It's better to ask 'what do I have to stop doing?'"'

After three years of studying the profiles of inspirational leaders and, at the same time, studying managers in the real world of work, we now hold somewhat provocative views. We now believe that it's easier and quicker to STOP doing the seven things that are demotivating our people than it is suddenly to pretend to be Jack Welch, Mother Teresa and Martin Luther King rolled into one. What started out as a light-hearted pun on the

Stephen Covey title *The Seven Habits of Highly Effective People* has become a serious call for action, because the impact of change is dramatic: you CAN inspire people to higher levels of perform-ance, productivity and profitability as long as you just STOP doing some or all of seven things.

How have we reached this conclusion? Well, in that coffee break about three years ago Steven unwittingly put his finger on something that had been bothering us for a while. And that something was this: that leadership development was increasing-ly being dominated by models of successful leaders, by case stud-ies and stories of high-achievers, and by shining examples of great leadership. We had written countless papers and had taught workshops round these themes many times. Our last book, *Leadership Unplugged,* was threaded through with case studies on the great leaders.

But we began to wonder how realistic it was to expect all the managers on our leadership development workshops to be able to emulate the great leaders? If we were genuinely interested in helping people to become authentic leaders, true to themselves and their beliefs, how could we ask them to copy other people, no matter how inspirational those role models were?

Secondly, we began to wonder if some of the case studies and examples of leaders we were using in business schools were simply too extreme, too 'inspirational', or simply too naive, for managers to consider seriously. This is especially true today when the mantra of the moment is the obsession with 'execution', 'JFDI', and 'boost this quarter's sales results'.

Unfortunately some managers are too short-sighted to see that people-focused leadership strategies do deliver performance, productivity and profitability. They choose to see people-focused strategies as too soft and not at all commercial. This is an enormous mistake and creates a huge self-fulfilling prophecy. 'Focusing on people,' goes the myth, 'means I can't be focusing on productivity and profitability. Therefore I shouldn't focus on people.' But by focusing on profit and a relentless drive towards sales these executives miss the essential intervening step – that it is people that deliver our profitability. Profit and performance are merely the outcomes of people-focused strategies, not a replacement for them.

'Keep your head down and look busy'

What many middle, junior and senior managers have told us in recent years is that, because of the short-term pressures they are under, they actually see the effort involved in becoming a better leader as either too unrealistic for their business situation or too much like hard work. 'Better to keep the head down and just look busy,' one cynical manager told us.

Yes, even after a huge investment of effort and money in leadership seminars, a significant number of people say they actually will not follow up at all. They will not undertake any of their so-called personal development plans, or indeed take any action at all.

After many encounters like this, we've begun to worry whether leadership development programmes that highlight only exemplary leaders may actually be causing harm to the goals of leadership development. Perhaps we are actually demotivating participants and sapping their confidence by setting aspirations that are far beyond what people are capable of achieving – through no fault of their own – because a kind of organizational leadenness weighs so heavy on them.

And this is another aspect of the great leader perspective that worries us. The rose-tinted view of most leadership research seems hugely at odds with the growing body of work on real life in companies. The real world of business has been captured with growing clarity, for instance, by the extensive work of the Gallup organisation. Gallup's research – described so vividly by Marcus Buckingham and Curt Coffman in *First, break all the rules* – clearly shows that people the world over are more likely to be disaffected, disengaged or demotivated by their managers than motivated or inspired.

So all of this together has prompted us to explore what actually can be achieved in practical and tangible terms by managers in their day-to-day roles. What could they do that would not involve major upheavals?

Well, this book has some powerful suggestions for you. So we urge you to set aside a few hours now to read the book once all the way through. Then come back to it and read it again, perhaps making notes in the margins. If you really mean to become an even better leader than you already are you owe it to yourself to make the effort.

Just stop doing seven things

After reviewing the motivational research of the last 20 years or so, and by comparing this with what participants in workshops and on our coaching programmes have told us over the past three years, it is very clear what managers can do. They can STOP doing just seven things. We've called them the Seven Failings of Really Useless Leaders. And the main body of this book explores the seven failings in detail.

We've run Seven Failings Workshops in Munich, Hong Kong, London and Atlanta over the past 18 months and the response has almost always been the same. Everywhere managers have told us their own examples of poor leadership from one or more of these categories. And when, in the workshops, we explain the underlying reasons behind the failings, the response is always one of disbelief and exasperation. 'If we've known about these failings for so long, why do we still experience them?' During the course of this book we'll explain as much as we can why we think the failings exist. And it isn't because most managers are fundamentally 'bad' bosses.

What can be done about the seven failings?

Of course, every manager is different, but broadly speaking we believe there is much for business schools and human resource professionals to do to overcome the seven failings in our firms.

1) Informal and offline development

First, it seems obvious, but if you're designing leadership development programmes, make sure there's plenty of informal and private time for discussions outside the formal classroom setting. Make sure there are empathetic faculty, tutors and coaches available for the discussions. An important goal of a leadership development event is to allow participants to explore their personal issues in settings outside the office and outside their family or social scene.

2) Use experiential development with action planning

Secondly, do make sure your leadership development activities get across or reinforce key theories and practical lessons about leadership – it's always worth reviewing the practical lessons that arise from motivation theories and goal theory, for instance.

Because today's leaders are much more educated than managers in the past there is much more to consider when designing development than simply to ensure all the 'knowledge' is addressed. So we need to make sure that there is enough experiential education in our developmental activities, from 360 degree surveys to 'Discovery' style or case study trips, to theatre work on physical presence and personal performance. What we increasingly need to communicate is less of an intellectual appreciation of the facts of leadership life, but more of the gut-wrenching certainty that people are important enough to do something about.

3) Use internal and external coaches and mentoring

One of the fastest growing issues for human resource professionals is the accelerating importance of coaching and mentoring, both by senior executives inside the firm and from outsiders. This is probably the fastest way to support development of effective leadership skills on the ground inside firms, but must be integrated with other development activities otherwise managers undergoing the coaching can feel isolated.

So, what is inspirational leadership?

Despite the light-hearted approach, smart managers will of course get the message – that inspirational leadership is about a number of key issues:

■ building on the natural enthusiasm of people in the team

■ empathising with people, and especially at the critical moments in their business career when they most need support

■ consistently communicating the vision and strategy for the business and where people fit in

■ focusing on the team, and on the team's objectives, ensuring that the team has as much input into those objectives as possible.

■ enticing people to perform well, with the right rewards for the right person in the right role

■ being sensitive to the culture or climate

■ and finally that it's about being scrupulously fair and constantly building trust within the team.

Cutting straight to the chase, you'll see that inspirational leadership is fundamentally about enthusiasm, empathy and energy. And if you focus your enthusiasm, empathy and energy relentlessly on your people, their performance, productivity and profitability will inevitably increase.

We look forward to working with you on this journey through the Seven Failings of Really Useless Leaders.

Jacqueline Moore
and Steven Sonsino
London, England
April 2007

Visit **7failings.com** *and click on*
FREE BOOK BONUSES
for additional resources

INTRODUCTION

Learning from failure and why it will help you

Why you must understand the 'failings' approach before you develop your inspirational leadership blueprint and just who is this book for?

THE QUESTIONS CAME FROM different ends of the world and when they came were something of a shock. There we were, engrossed in writing articles for various magazines and making short films about the seven failings, and on the same day we had two questions that stopped us in our tracks.

The first question came in an interview with Alison Hjul, the Research Director for Webster Buchanan, an international HR consultancy based in California. She asked Steven 'Why are you studying failure when all the prevailing wisdom says to concentrate on being positive and helping people to identify and play to their strengths?'

It's a great question and one that we really want to address for you here. Because, yes, positive psychology tells us that we need to help people focus on their strengths as opposed to failings. But identifying the Seven Failings of Really Useless Leaders doesn't mean we've turned our back on positive psychology. To explain what we mean, we'd like to recommend a somewhat unusual book to you.

One of the most surprising leadership books we've ever come across, full of valuable practical advice, is Sandra Gookin's *Parenting for Dummies*. In the book, Gookin makes the point very well about the importance of being positive. When parents talk with their children, she says, they often concentrate on what children should not do or what they should not touch. But this only signals to children that if they do 'those' things or touch 'that' then they will get some attention.

So when mum or dad says 'don't touch' they are in effect daring a child to touch. And, when the child inevitably 'misbehaves', the payoff is instant and the child gets the attention he or she was looking for. OK, it's not very nice attention – but it is attention nevertheless.

Instead of this vicious cycle, focused as it is on poor behaviour, says Gookin, we should 'catch them doing something right'. We love this approach. Catch them doing something right. You see, positive feedback lets people know that they're doing something helpful or useful. There's an important bonus, too: if what we're telling them about is something the person does very well, we're signalling to people what their natural strengths are. We are also signalling that we value those skills and actions. For many people, knowing that others value what they do can be a major confidence booster. 'I'll do that again, then,' is the usual reaction.

Now, of course, adults do differ from children, but the psychological foundations of positive feedback are broadly similar in both. The point, at least, is well made – we should offer positive feedback to adults as well as children. And is it any wonder, with children or adults, that when good behaviour, useful behaviour or valued behaviour gets noticed it gets repeated? This is the classic win-win situation of positive feedback. Catch them doing something right.

From this perspective, we are making a big mistake with this book. Clearly we are identifying failings and it is these failings that people are likely to repeat in the future. But we believe we haven't made a mistake. We see no paradox in supporting a positive psychology approach at the same time as identifying the Seven Failings of Really Useless Leaders. And here's the main reason.

If we can help you simply to stop certain misguided actions, that we've identified as the Seven Failings, by default your natural inspirational behaviour will shine through. The upshot of this is that you'll get better business results. In fact, it's these better results that we're betting on. If you can get more productivity, more performance and more profitability from your people, we believe you're more likely to want to stop the 'old' behaviour and continue with the 'new' behaviour. And then you'll discover that delivering better results by NOT using the failings is closer to what we'd call your natural style. You will evolve an authentic, positive leadership style that delivers far better business results.

At the risk of over-using the 'psychology' word, perhaps we should describe our approach as a kind of reverse psychology. We're apparently concentrating on leadership failings, while focusing in reality on how to become a better inspirational leader.

To be honest, though, if we'd called this book 'How to be an inspirational leader' it would have sounded a bit pompous. It probably wouldn't have received as much attention as it has, either. But 'The Seven Failings' doesn't work as the title of a workshop. Not many people want to go to a programme called the 'Seven Failings of Really Useless Leaders' – it sounds too much like a prison sentence for poor managers than something of real benefit. So that's why we call the associated workshop our Inspirational Leadership Blueprint Seminar. Let's face it. Would you show up at an hotel in Miami, Berlin or London saying 'Could you tell me where the Seven Failings of Really Useless Leaders workshop is?' No, much better for you to say 'I'm here for the Inspirational Leadership Blueprint Seminar'.

What's new and what can you learn?

We had just put the phone down after the call with Alison Hjul at Webster Buchanan when another tricky question was thrown at us – this time on a blog. We'd been working with German companies including Sony Ericsson and Deutsche Bank for some time, so *Focus* magazine in Germany did a major interview with Steven after one Seven Failings workshop in Munich.

We concluded the interview one morning over a traditional German breakfast. The discussion went well and a few days later the interview was posted on the *Focus* website. In the blog over the next few days many supportive comments were posted, mainly on how widespread the Seven Failings still were – unfortunately. But there was one question that left us distraught when we were reviewing the blog that day. 'What's new?' said one anonymous writer. 'There's nothing in the Seven Failings that's new,' they said. 'We've known about these for years.'

We were distraught when we got this message. But not because the writer was wrong. They were absolutely on target – none of the Seven Failings is new in itself. No, we were distraught because we had fallen at the first hurdle. 'What's new?' is the key question every academic has to answer when they're publishing their research. And we hadn't made it clear that it isn't the Seven Failings themsleves that are news. The news is the fact that the Seven Failings still occur today in the behaviour of managers and the fact that they are still so widespread.

So why do the Seven Failings still exist when we've known about them for so long? Why do leaders use the Seven Failings rather than inspirational leadership behaviour?

We believe that the Seven Failings are things we've learned over the years – they've become habits that are really hard to shake. Some of the habits are drawn from our early experience of family life, some from our experience of school life and some from our early work experience. And they've stuck with us. We'll say more about this in a later chapter.

So our aim with this book is to help you to jettison the Seven Failings in favour of your natural leadership style. We'll explain to you how your mental blueprint probably evolved and offer you tactics and strategies to change your mental map for the better. And when we do this, you are likely to become a better, more authentic leader, delivering better business and personal results.

In short, we'd like to suggest that this is not a book about learning. It's a book about unlearning. It's about unlearning the things holding you back rather than a book about learning a stack of new things to do. And we want to say some more about unlearning now.

The three real reasons you need this book

There are two reasons why you might need this book and one key reason why you've never come across anything quite like this before. Let's look at the first reason – which we call the 'mere mortals' fallacy.

In one of Steven's early leadership workshops at Cranfield School of Management he had been discussing Gandhi with people from a global telecommunications firm. He had been using segments from Richard Attenborough's Oscar-winning movie about the life and death of Gandhi and had broken for tea at the end of one afternoon segment. A man came over and he was obviously moved by the discussion and by watching the clips from the movie. His jaw was clenched and he was tightening and untightening his fists. He obviously wanted to say something, but nothing was coming out. He scratched his forehead, settled his glasses on the bridge of his nose. Then he swallowed loudly and blurted out 'I just can't be Gandhi. I'm just a … we're all just … mere mortals. How can I lead like that?' And he pointed to the screen behind his head.

It was the first time we'd heard this comment, but it certainly wasn't the last. We've come to know this as 'the mere mortals fallacy'. The idea that when it comes to the 'superleaders' – JFK, Martin Luther King, Churchill, Mother Teresa – we just can't learn from them because… well, they're just too different from ordinary people, larger than life, out of the ordinary.

The mere mortals fallacy is a clear reminder, actually, that our work in teaching is not just to say 'watch this', 'read those' or 'try that'. A major part of our role as professors is to help people explore what the lessons of life actually mean for them. We need to help our clients and customers to realise that we're not asking them to copy these amazing people. We need to help people to learn again. To review, critically analyse and then apply the relevant lessons. What this has helped us as authors to realise is that maybe we all – as adult humans, full of our certainties and egos – have forgotten how to be open to new ideas. We truly have forgotten how to learn.

So it's probably no surprise that we now show fewer movie clips and discuss the lives of 'great leaders' far less. We spend *some* time looking at how a Jack Welch or an Anita Roddick made their choices. But we prefer to spend most of the time in seminars and workshops looking at what our participants think, at what you think about your day-to-day actions in the office or in your life. We want to urge you to reflect on what you believe in, fundamentally, about leadership and how you aim to make that come to life in your own words and actions.

So the first reason you might need this book is if you've ever felt that you 'couldn't be a Gandhi'. And the first thing we'll respond with is 'don't worry'. We don't want you to be. However, you can still learn from the lives of great leaders, so don't completely ignore what Gandhi and the inspirational role models like him can teach us.

The second reason you need this book is if you're struggling with what we've come to call the cod liver oil effect.

Steven had been invited to give the keynote speech at the annual general meeting of the Institute of Chartered Accountants. The event filled the Great Hall of the beautiful headquarters of the Institute, in the heart of the City of London. Steven asked the audience how many of them would like to be healthier. Almost everyone raised a hand in the air. (Some people raised both hands.) After a brief pause, Steven offered the audience … cod liver oil capsules. He produced a jumbo carton from his briefcase like a rabbit from a hat. Unfortunately there were no takers. No one volunteered to take a cod liver oil capsule, though everyone knew it would make them 'healthier'.

Then Steven explained that this always happens. No one – usually – was willing to take the action needed to get better or healthier. Consuming the capsules was always considered to be 'too much effort', or 'distasteful'. Of course, taking vitamins or healthy supplements is not always the way to get healthy, but the point was made.

Many managers report that they are under so much pressure, are so short staffed, or just have so much to do that they can't be concerned with becoming better managers or leaders. No, they don't want to take the cod liver oil capsule of leadership development. They just don't have time.

There is another group of managers who are actually too modest, and perhaps less assertive than other managers. These managers put their own needs last in the list of priorities. 'I have to serve my clients, my colleagues and my boss first. That leaves no time for me or my needs.' They don't take the cod liver oil capsule of leadership development because they put their own needs last, perhaps not realising that their boss, their colleagues and their customers would actually benefit if they became better leaders.

Then there are the managers who, if they're honest, are a little insecure in their work role. Business is tough, there are competitors circling like sharks and fear in the workplace is tangible. These managers are insecure and they don't want to take the cod liver oil capsule of leadership development either. What they are concerned with, above everything else, is simply avoiding failure. Avoiding pain. (If this describes you, perhaps this book could be an important painkiller.)

If you fall into one or other of these groups, then maybe that's what attracted you to the Seven Failings approach. Perhaps you want to lead in a more inspirational way, but it seems like too much effort, or you're putting yourself at the bottom of the heap, or you just want to keep out of the limelight.

Whatever your reasons for avoiding the cod liver oil capsule of leadership development we will take you through our step-by-step approach to developing an Inspirational Leadership Blueprint. We can help you to lead in a different way. We can help you to become more inspirational and to deliver better results, but no, you don't have to do anything. We're just asking you to stop doing one or more of seven things.

There's one final reason why, we believe, you probably haven't come across anything like this book and this approach before. And it's this. Much of what our profession does is to flatter the executives and managers who are our customers. Sometimes as consultants and educators we collude with managers in the pretence that they're 'actually quite good managers'. We do believe, though, that it's done with the best possible end in mind. We flatter executives in the hope that we can then help them, in tactful and subtle ways, to appreciate that there are better ways to manage and lead.

But outside the seminar room, outside the consulting engagement, isn't it possible to talk about poor management and poor leadership openly from time to time? At the risk of upsetting a few people here, we have to report that sometimes it feels like we're trapped in the fable of the Emperor's new clothes, that we're the only ones running through the streets saying 'Look at the King! Look at the King!' You don't see many consultants or academics on the streets of the business world saying 'Look at the King!' And it's easy to see why.

If you accept that the consulting and professional development industries work mainly by flattering senior executives—and usually we're very subtle about this—then understanding why is fairly straightforward. We need their support because we engage them in support for our research. We write case studies about successful leaders. We write books and biographies about successful leaders. But much of this work is written looking backwards over a project or over a manager's career. It's often a post-rationalised, re-written, re-scripted history.

From a senior executive's point of view this makes perfect sense. Who wouldn't want to be captured for posterity as a strong, decisive leader? On the other hand, who would want to be captured forever in print as someone who was NOT a good leader? As someone who didn't know what was going on? As someone who failed? We can't think of many examples, can you? Very few executives have that courage and much of the real world is kept securely off-the-record. To be brutally honest, while it sells very well in airport bookstalls, much of the great leader literature is of little use in real practical terms. (Great stories though. Good entertainment.)

So in part this book is a nod in the direction of the real world of work, red in tooth and claw. We believe that poor leadership is far more common than most professionals are prepared to admit in public. And our conclusion? We think that all of us should take a new look at our own leadership style before we criticise the skills and style of our colleagues or peers or bosses. Let's take an honest look in the mirror before we get strange ideas about how brilliant we are as leaders. Let's be prepared to be a little vulnerable here and say 'no, I don't have all the answers', or 'no, I don't know', or 'no, I can't manage on my own', or 'yes, I need help'.

Do you have the courage to be honest about your own leadership skills? If the answer is yes, then maybe this book can help.

Steven gets called many things by our clients and customers, but someone quite recently bowled up to him at the end of an afternoon seminar and said, with a smile playing on their face, 'You're actually a "professor of harsh reality" aren't you?' 'Better than being a professor of pipedreams,' Steven replied.

So who should read this book?

While we were putting this book together, our US coaches Randy Gilbert and Peggy McColl urged us to be explicit about exactly who the readers would be and what kind of audience the book would be valuable for. 'Be specific,' they said. 'Describe the kinds of jobs people do and what their daily life is like.'

We've found this difficult. It's difficult to be explicit about job titles, for instance, because people at very different levels in companies seem to be facing the kinds of challenge that we've uncovered. People at middle, junior and senior levels in business have all revealed to us their leadership challenges, and they are challenges based on frustration. So we've decided to write this section – who the book is for – based on those challenges people have shared with us.

We believe that the book – and the video programmes and workshops that accompany the book – are going to be most of value to executives who are tired of throwing all their leadership effort into generating short-term returns only to watch morale, team performance and productivity drain away while financial profitability barely covers their expenses.

This book will help you if you want to increase your team's productivity and profitability year after year and if you want to keep your business costs under control and practically eliminate poor customer service and complaints.

It will help you if you're finding that, instead of rising each year, your profitability falls a little more each quarter. Perhaps you're spending more cash to generate fewer sales. And the increasing numbers of last-minute lost sales mean you're never sure until the last day of the quarter whether you will be profitable or not.

What's worse is that the more you focus on the short-term

because performance is drying up, the prospects for your next career move also seem to evaporate.

If you want foolproof tactics and strategies for injecting more energy and performance into your team ... while actually spending less of your day hand-holding everyone all the time... then you're likely to find things that you can learn from and do here.

Are you motivated to tackle these challenges?

Let us issue a small health warning, however. You will most benefit from our approach if you're motivated to tackle these challenges. If you want to spend more of your working hours doing what a leader really does – leading – while at the same time preparing for your next career step.

And while you're motivated to tackle these situations, you're most likely frustrated and we know the frustration you're feeling because we've struggled with this, too. We've managed creative and spirited teams of professionals in the media industry, only to have their edge blunted by short-termism and a broad mis-understanding of people management.

What happened? Well, in one situation the board urged us to focus exclusively on short-term profitability and cost-cutting at the expense of everything else. Morale and performance were shattered. In another case the company spiralled into a six-month industrial dispute that almost destroyed it.

It isn't just established large multinationals that suffer, though, when it comes to performance, productivity and profitability. We've struggled with the challenges of launching entrepreneurial businesses, too. Both of us went without sleep for weeks while we were launching an exciting new internet business – but we couldn't get people pulling together in the same way.

That little disaster cost us personally hundreds of thousands of pounds in real terms and in lost income. It also put our careers back a few years. But it did teach us a huge amount about what we believe in and about what is the right way to lead and inspire people.

How much change can you embrace?

We know many managers who were once where you are right now. They became directors and managers years ago because they wanted to control their own destiny. But today some of them still work terrible hours, and are virtual slaves to their executive boards or their clients. Many struggle to get the visibility or the credit they deserve inside or outside the company. Most have precious little personal freedom.

For these men and women, becoming a senior manager was in reality a chore instead of a joy. You can imagine that some have developed skin or stomach disorders from all the stress.

You may be wondering: what keeps them tied to their jobs? The money is all right most of the time. In many cases it's actually rather good. But at other times the financial return hardly seems to balance the physical and emotional effort of going to work.

Shouldn't being a senior manager be different? We think so. And, if we're right about you, you do as well. But only if you're prepared to work at making a change.

When Steven was choosing between different business schools when he wanted to do an MBA he found most of them were very professional, thorough in what they professed and very clear about what they offered. But the thing that really captured his attention was a question. that Martyn Jones, an upright, ex-Army officer who was then Director of the MBA at Cranfield

School of Management, asked. 'He asked me how much change I was prepared to embrace,' says Steven. 'It got me thinking.'

This seems a good moment for us to ask you … how much change are you prepared to embrace? It's a serious question, so take a few moments to reflect on your answer. How much change are you prepared to embrace?

What is in this book?

So what is in this book? More management theories to add to your kitbag of tools? Well, no. You actually don't need any more theory about leadership or how to lead people. Most managers are full to the back teeth with management theories. What you need is a street-smart system that will help you to:

■ lead your business,
■ slash unnecessary costs,
■ and keep customers so pumped up about you that they become ambassadors and evangelists, helping you to reap more and better sales.

Of course, the system needs to be based on theories that have been rigorously tested and tried in practice over years if not decades. It's a favourite saying in academic circles that there's nothing as practical as a good theory.

Until recently, however, the only way to discover the practical nature of management theory was through painful, time-consuming and profit-devouring trial and error. But now you can master the nuts and bolts of a practical leadership system based on rigorous management thinking by reading just this one book. You can learn from all the mistakes that we've made and all the lessons we've learned along the way without going into all the jargon, or the never ending background and references of a highly theoretical text.

In this book we'll reveal to you the Seven Failings of Really Useless Leaders and how we have translated these into our Inspirational Leadership Blueprint, with the lessons all presented in a step-by-step system you can begin to use the minute you turn the last page.

You see, over the last three years we've spent thousands of hours and thousands of pounds to figure out how the Inspirational Leadership Blueprint fits together. And now we're ready to share it with you. The Inspirational Leadership Blueprint is a system that you can use to:

■ create a team of productive people who deliver huge productivity, performance and profitability for you and your company
■ build a leadership reputation in your industry and attract the best performers to you like a magnet
■ get approached by dozens of people who are your ideal clients and customers.

Now we believe we've got it. We've got this all down to a complete system that we want to pass on to those people who want outstanding leadership success in their career. So if you want to take your career to the next level, we have three powerful ingredients for you in the Inspirational Leadership Blueprint:

■ essential leadership knowledge
■ critical commercial insight
■ and superb motivational skill.

And while we've been very good at teaching people parts of

this system in the past, we've never really connected all the dots for people. We've never before put it all together and given away all our secrets.

So that's what you're holding in your hands. All the practical leadership secrets that will help you to become an even more inspirational leader – not by doing new and different things, but by stopping the seven things that are holding you back in your business and career.

What we'll tackle next is the most important idea behind the Seven Failings of Really Useless Leaders: your Inspirational Leadership Blueprint. What are the things that condition you to lead the way you do and can you change your leadership style if it isn't working for you?

Your Inspirational Leadership Blueprint

Is your Inspirational Leadership Blueprint set for success?
And, if not, how can you change it so that it is?

Tom Ryan is a finance wizard. He's tall and slim, he's Irish and he's fanatical about golf. Tom shared an office with Steven for about a year before taking the reins as Director of the Centre for Management Development at London Business School. And he would often draw his stories from the game of golf.

'Leadership is just like the inner game of golf,' Tom says. 'You can have all the clubs and strokes and tools that you like, but unless your inner game, your inner self, is set for success you don't stand a chance on the fairway.'

So before we get into the detail on the Seven Failings of Really Useless Leaders, this is what we want to cover in this section, the inner game of leadership. We call it your Inspirational Leadership Blueprint and in this section we want to ask you the question 'Is your inspirational leadership blueprint set for success?' You see, if the outer game of leadership is all about business knowledge, skills and strategies, the inner game is just as essential. It's about you, your leadership experience to date and your level of leadership confidence.

Steven has a saying in his seminars: 'It's not enough to be in the right place at the right time. You have to be the right person in the right place at the right time.' So who are you, actually? How do you think? What do you really feel about yourself? How confident are you in your abilities? How well do you relate to other people? How much do you trust people? What is your ability to act in spite of any fear you might be feeling? And can you act when you're just not in the mood?

The truth of the matter is that your character and the habitual things you do, the things you routinely think, are a critical part of what determines your leadership success. And at this point in the book you should have come to the realisation that your leadership success can only grow to the extent that you do.

Inspirational Leadership Blueprint Principle

**Your leadership success can grow
only to the extent that you do –
So how much are you prepared
to grow and develop?**

Have you ever been to a meeting, or even to a workshop or seminar, and taken pages of notes only to forget everything that was said or covered almost completely? You're not alone. There is so much information today clamouring for your attention that any new information has to be really special to get in.

Marketers and PR professionals can twist the words 'really special' to mean a huge variety of things. But for us the phrase 'really special' means that the information has high WIIFM value. WIIFM, of course, is 'What's In It For Me?'

In other words, we explain 'really special' in one of two ways:

*1) Really special information directly affects you **financially***

*2) Or really special information directly affects you **emotionally**.*

And that's what we want to touch on here for a moment.

In our seminars we draw on many learning techniques to accelerate your learning and to allow you to 'experience' as well as hear our messages. These 'experiential learning' techniques help you to get the point more quickly and to remember more of what you learn. The key word for us is 'participation'. Participating actively in your personal development can help you to absorb key messages more effectively and make important new additions to your collection of beliefs. You can even edit or delete old beliefs that no longer work for you. But you have to work at it. So we encourage you to involve yourself in your development, even while you're reading this book, because what you only hear or see in passing you will forget.

So from time to time in this book we'll highlight a key message as a Blueprint Principle like the one on the opposite page. And we're going to ask you to write it down and take a moment to think about what it means for you. We'll also add some questions from time to time that we want you to reflect on and answer.

Please don't skip this task. The more you explore these issues and how they could apply in your own life and work, the more likely it is that you will be prompted to do something or do something differently as a result of working with us through these pages. If you don't do anything after reading this book then you're simply wasting your time. And we think that, having come this far, you do want to make an impact on your personal performance, your productivity and your profitability. You do want to reach your full leadership potential, don't you?

Do you want to reach your full potential?

The sad reality is that most people never reach their full potential. Most people simply stop developing their skills and style, believing either that they know it all or that 'you can't teach an old dog new tricks'. The real reason, in our view, is that they're unconscious. A little asleep at the wheel. Though they may be smart, at an intellectual level, they lead their teams only at a fairly superficial level – based only on what they can see. They live strictly in the visible world. We believe that there's much more to human nature. Like the iceberg that has 90% of its mass beneath the surface, we too have most of what makes us up beneath the surface.

So we suggest that you need to become more expert at uncovering what's beneath the surface in your business relationships. In other words, we want you to bear in mind that your personal performance as a leader is driven not only by your mental skills or intellect. It is also driven by your social skills, what has come to be known in part as emotional intelligence made popular by Daniel Goleman in the 1990s[2]. We'll deal with this in detail later in the book.

It's also worth remembering that what people make of your values, what they think your values are, is incredibly important. Notice that we didn't say what values you 'actually' hold, or what values you 'say' you hold. We mean what values people 'think' you hold. You see, we sometimes forget, in all our relations with other people, that perception is reality. Their perception of us is their reality. In other words, people relate to us based on how they think we are. If they believe we are unapproachable, they won't approach us. (Even if actually we're only shy.) If they believe we will criticise their ideas, they won't come to us with ideas. (Even if actually we are only clumsy in how we discuss possible improvements.)

Indeed, of the three aspects of our make-up – our intellect, our social skills and our values – it is what people make of our values that is the most important. How do we walk the leadership talk?

The next piece of the puzzle to think about is implementation, to an extent. If you have ever wondered how to raise someone's performance, or the productivity of a team, or the profitability of a business, then you have to be concerned with all three levels of your own leadership blueprint. Yes, your leadership programming must be reviewed and perhaps changed at all three levels – the intellectual level, the emotional level and the ethical or values level.

This is because we live in a world of cause and effect. And when you have a problem with the performance of your team, for example, you have to recognise that you are seeing a symptom of a deeper problem. You're seeing a symptom of what's going on underneath the surface in you.

This is because whatever results you are getting – good or bad, positive or negative, profitable or unprofitable – depends on what's happening for you on the inside. You've got to remember that the physical or visible world is simply a reflection of what's going on in the inner world of your Inspirational Leadership Blueprint. Getting back to the game of golf, if things aren't going well in the outer game, it's because things aren't going well in your inner game. It's that simple.

What is an Inspirational Leadership Blueprint?

Professor Andrew Kakabadse is an impressive man. Broad shouldered, powerful, always relaxed. He walks purposefully, one hand in his pocket, the other carrying his diary on a strap, continental style. And whenever he speaks people listen. Early on when you meet him he is likely to highlight some of his experience from the world of family therapy, but he applies this to great effect in the executive world as a Professor of International Management Development. He works up close and personal with senior executives on interpersonal relationships among other things.

Perhaps the most impressive thing he does is analyse where people are as leaders. 'Give me five minutes,' he says, 'and I can identify your personal leadership challenges.'

You might be wondering how he does this. The answer is, basically, in a short conversation. With just a few questions, Andrew identifies the underpinning beliefs you have about people, about yourself and about how relationships work.

This, in a nutshell, is what we have come to call your Inspirational Leadership Blueprint. Each of us has a blueprint already embedded in our subconscious mind. And this, more than anything else, determines your leadership success.

What is an Inspirational Leadership Blueprint? Well, like the blueprint for a skyscraper or a house it is a preset design or plan. It defines the way you intend to manage or lead in particular situations. It consists of the complete combination of thoughts, feelings and actions that you hold about leadership.

How is it formed? Well, that's simple. The blueprint is formed mainly from the information or programming you received in the past. For instance, much of our make-up is influenced by the relationships we forged as children and young adults. The blueprint is also influenced in our formative years, when we learned our professional skills and in your formative first few years at work.

Now, although this blueprint is influenced when we change roles or companies, it's fairly stable over time. So an important question to consider is who were the main sources of your leadership programming or conditioning? Where did your programming come from?

The list, of course, includes parents, our brothers and sisters and our first friends. Then there are the authority figures that come later: school teachers, professional trainers and your early bosses. And it is this unique combination of people in your past that has conditioned you, leaving you with a set of automatic leadership responses that will run unchecked for the rest of your life. Unless, of course, you intervene and revise your leadership blueprint. This is exactly what we will do with this book, if you're up for the challenge. And we also do this in more detail during our Inspirational Leadership Blueprint Seminar, on a deeper and more permanent level.

What impact does conditioning have on you?

Like any computing machine, your mind is conditioned or programmed to work in a certain way. The conditioning leads to certain thoughts in you. Your thoughts lead to feelings. Your feelings then prompt you to take certain actions and your actions deliver results. So the overall impact of your prior conditioning can be mapped like this:

$$C \rightarrow T \rightarrow F \rightarrow A = R$$

Inspirational Leadership
Blueprint Principle

Conditioning leads to thoughts
Thoughts lead to feelings
Feelings lead to actions
Actions lead to results

So to change the results you get,
you need to change your conditioning

From this sequence, we're sure you can appreciate that the first step to changing your results is therefore to change your programming. In a sense we are again asking you to unlearn some of the unhelpful things you might have incorporated into your way of leading.

How are you conditioned?

Before you can influence or revise your programming or conditioning, you have to understand in some detail exactly how you are conditioned. And conditioning takes place fundamentally in three ways:

■ *Verbal programming* What did you *hear* in your early adult life?
■ *Role models* What did you *see* when you were a young leader?
■ *Specific incidents or experience* What did you *experience* on the first rungs of your management career?

These three aspects of conditioning are so important to

understand we need to go over each of them here briefly. When you've got a sense of the three forms of conditioning, you can then begin to unravel the elements that aren't working as successfully as they could be for you.

The first influence: verbal programming

Let's begin with the verbal programming you've received. What did you hear about leading people when you were growing up? Tick the phrases that you've heard:

'Because I say so'	❏
'You have to tell people exactly what to do'	❏
'Leave your personal life at home'	❏
'Give them an inch and they'll take a mile'	❏
'There's no place for emotions in decision making'	❏
'I'm the boss'	❏
'Work is for work'	❏
'Unless you tell people what to do they just waste their time'	❏
'You can't trust anybody'	❏

(If you really want a poke in the eye, now go back and tick again all the phrases you've ever **heard yourself say.** Like parents with their growing children, sometimes we as managers say things we swore we would never say, or do things we swore we would never do. This is another example of how trapped we are by our own past experience.)

Here's the point: every statement you ever heard about leading people, or how difficult people are, or how much they need to be controlled, remains in your subconscious mind as part of the leadership blueprint that is running your leadership style. And if the statements were made by influential people, like your parents, your friends or your first boss, then the conditioning becomes very deeply anchored. It's difficult for us to believe that our parents or friends or our early bosses were wrong. They are successful people after all.

Verbal conditioning is extremely powerful. If you have children you'll know that children pick up and copy the phrases their parents use. We were astounded, for instance, when we asked our son Christopher what he'd like to drink and he came right back with the phrase 'I wouldn't mind a cappuccino.' He was three.

**Inspirational Leadership
Blueprint Principle**

**When the subconscious mind must choose
between logic and deeply rooted emotions,
the emotions will almost always win**

Of course, you also hear other elements of verbal programming, like 'be nice to your brother' and 'say "thank you"', which we accept logically will get better behaviour (and performance) out of people. But when the subconscious mind has to choose between logic and deeply rooted emotions, then the emotions will almost always win.

As with all attempts to change things there are a number of stages you need to go through to recondition or reprogramme your leadership blueprint. They may seem basic, but if you follow these simple steps you will notice yourself becoming more aware of the tiniest things and better able to change what you're doing.

The steps are simple but profoundly powerful:

1) STOP Become aware
2) ANALYSE Increase understanding
3) REFLECT Break the cycle
4) START Craft new intentions

The first step on the road to change is **awareness**. You can't change something unless you know it exists and that it is causing you problems.

The second part of change is **increasing your understanding**. If you can begin to understand where your thinking comes from, you can recognise that the elements that may not be working for you have come from outside you.

The third element of change involves **breaking the cycle**. Once you realise that a particular way of thinking hasn't come from you, you can separate or dissociate yourself from it and choose whether to keep it or let it go.

The final element of change is **reconditioning**. We spend most of our time on the Inspirational Leadership Blueprint Workshop developing new skills for the future because over a longer period of time we can introduce you to new ways of generating productivity and performance in your people through your reinvented leadership style.

So if you want to take this further we invite you to attend the Inspirational Leadership Blueprint Seminar where you will be led through a mixture of informational and experiential techniques that will rewire your subconscious mind, retraining you to respond supportively in terms of your inspirational leadership style.

In our research and testing of the Inspirational Leadership

Blueprint our good friends Steve Berry, of Neos Learning, Jules Goddard from London Business School, Christian Anderson from Deutsche Bank and Steve Anderson, formerly CIO with Davis Langdon, have emphasised the importance of ongoing help and support. These are essential for long-lasting change to occur. So apart from the templates and ideas in this book we have another free gift to help you here.

If you go to **www.7failings.com** and click on "FREE BOOK BONUSES" you can subscribe to the Inspirational Leadership Blueprint "thought of the week". Every seven days you will receive a short but profound lesson that can help you on your journey to greater leadership success.

Before we move on to the next step let's recap on our discussion of verbal programming and the steps you need to take now to begin reconditioning your Inspirational Leadership Blueprint.

Steps For Change: Verbal programming

STOP (awareness)

Write down all the statements and phrases you heard in the past about leaders, leadership, leading, and managing people.

THINK (understanding)

Take each statement and write down how you believe it has affected your leadership style so far.

ANALYSE (break the cycle)

How might these statements not be helpful to you in managing or leading others? What have others told you about your leadership style? What have you read in books or heard in seminars about leadership that differs from the statements you've written down? Where are the contradictions with the statements you've listed above? Which statements do you find somewhat suspect on reflection?

START (recondition)

Which of the statements you started with can you say are not necessarily true for you? What new statements can you adopt or use to influence a new way of leading? What are you prepared to start believing or doing?

Go to the Seven Failings website at **www.7failings.com** *and go to* **FREE BOOK BONUSES** *to download all our* **'Steps For Change'** *templates*

The second influence: role models

The second way we are conditioned, and an equally powerful one, is by the role models we are exposed to. What were your parents or guardians like as leaders? Did one or both of them set a good example, or not? Were they risk takers or conservative? How collaborative were they? What about your teachers? Were they somewhat inspirational or simply dictatorial? And your early bosses, in part-time work during your teenage years and even as a young adult?

Now you've probably already guessed why this is important. You see, we tend to copy the folks we've been exposed to. In some ways, because we only see one style of manager, we assume that is the only way to manage. This is especially true for those people who spend a long time in one job or in one company or working for one manager. Never exposed to another style or another way of working you become programmed to respond in certain ways.

This is of course related to company culture – the way we do things round here – and it's extremely hard to shake. The ritual or routine habits that we get into, and especially the bad habits that we get into.

So consider this – what habits do you have that might be hindering your ability to motivate and inspire your people? What do you regularly do that depresses the energy of your people and reduces their ability or willingness to perform at a higher level for you?

One of the saddest things we've uncovered is that sometimes people even know that what they're doing is not helpful. But they just can't kick the habit. It's what Jeffrey Pfeffer and Bob Sutton at Stanford Business School call the 'knowing-doing' gap. We know what to do – we're just not doing it. And the important question is why? Well, we'll give you our take on that later in the book.

But for now let's tell you the story of Petra who attended one of our seminars and was struggling with a couple of things. 'When I was a member of the team with a boss who kept checking up on everything we were doing I felt demotivated and drained of energy. It wasn't a good way to manage, I thought.' But then Petra was promoted to manager of the team and she was stunned. 'I managed in exactly the same way. And the team seemed to expect it of me.'

Because Petra had only ever experienced this controlling style of management she knew no other way to operate. And while she realised she was demotivating her people, there was nothing she could do to change her way of working. 'What really trapped me in this way of working is that the team almost seemed to expect me to behave in this way. They waited for me to check their work before making any forward progress.'

When we explored with Petra what were the driving forces behind the style she had adopted she began to realise that as well as not having had a positive role model in recent times she also wanted to be seen as a tough manager, just like the previous boss. 'I wanted to live up to my promotion. I wanted people to know or think that I had been promoted for a reason. So I had to act like a big boss,' she said.

Inspirational Leadership
Blueprint Principle

If you are worried about looking weak, or if you need to prove yourself with your people or your bosses, then your leadership will never be truly inspirational

But let's also introduce a second point here, a second principle on this subject.

Inspirational Leadership
Blueprint Principle

Whatever we do, however we lead, we are
a role model for our people.

So how can you be the best you can be,
a brilliant role model?

Clearly what needs to happen is for you to unlink your motivation with success from insecurity, fear or anger. You need to dissociate your need to succeed from your need to be seen as a good or tough leader. What you will then be doing is replacing your faulty thinking with new thinking that more nearly matches your personal style. You will be thinking about your contribution and purpose. What can I uniquely bring? What value do I personally add?

Importantly you will also realise that you don't need to copy anyone else – something we discussed earlier.

Let's make a short summary of these points here.

Steps For Change: Role models

STOP (awareness)
Consider the different ways of leading that you have seen or witnessed. Write down how you may lead in an identical or different way.

THINK (understanding)
Take each element of the leadership styles you have seen and write down how you believe each has affected your own leadership style so far.

ANALYSE (break the cycle)
Can you see how these ways of leading may not be helpful to you in managing or leading others? What have others told you about your leadership style? What can you learn from that feedback? Can you see that you have a choice about how you manage or lead in the future? What might you begin to change if you had the time or strength or commitment?

START (recondition)
Which of the statements you started with can you say are not necessarily true for you? What new statements can you adopt, what new behaviour can you model to influence a new way of leading? What are you prepared to start believing or doing?

Go to the Seven Failings website at **www.7failings.com** *and go to* **FREE BOOK BONUSES** *to download all our* **'Steps For Change'** *templates*

The third influence: specific incidents and your experience
The third main way that we are conditioned or programmed is through our own personal experience. What specific things happened to us in our formative years that shaped the way we manage or lead people. These experiences are among the most powerful we ever have because they act as a crucible that forges and shapes the beliefs and illusions we come to live by.

Take a moment now to review the incidents and events of your own experience. Where are the moments that most influenced your leadership style? It might be a situation where an authority figure such as a parent, teacher or boss has communicated something intensely to you through an experience. This could be the importance of 'do what you're told' when you suffered the consequences of not doing what you're told. It could be the importance of 'sell more now' and you didn't sell enough. It could be that your boss's mantra is 'don't make mistakes' and through no fault of your own you made a mistake.

Moments where you experienced some consequence for what was regarded as 'poor performance' are often very influential in defining our style.

Reflecting on the specific incidents that influenced us is an important task. And it's also worth reflecting on the fact that all of us have different experiences. We lead in different ways because we had different experiences when we were younger. So even though you may work on the same team as someone else, and you think you know them, you would probably be surprised at the different way they see leadership.

Why is this important? Well, we know that if your leadership blueprint doesn't match the blueprint of the person you're dealing with then you could have a major challenge.

The trick is to realise that you're dealing with a difference in blueprints and people's beliefs not a difference in 'people'. And once you begin to recognise what shape someone's blueprint takes, you can begin to work with it, to identify their hopes and fears, and provide the right kind of motivation and inspiration.

One of the most important things you'll do if you choose to attend the Inspirational Leadership Blueprint Seminar is learn how to recognize the blueprints that other people hold and how to work together with them to define new blueprints – held by both of you. This will help you as partners in a business relationship to get what you want from each other. It's powerful to do this as it relieves a big causes of tension – misunderstanding.

One of the things you can begin to do with the people on your team – or with your peers or bosses actually – is to sit down and discuss the history that you each have, as far as leadership experience is concerned. Who were your key role models? What did you learn from each of them? What formative experiences did you go through that helped shape your thinking?

Also, find out what leadership or leadership success, really means for your team and for your boss. Is it security or status? Is it financial success? A greater purpose in life? More freedom? What exactly? This will help you in your day-to-day relationships with them and may help you discover why you might be disagreeing in the business arena.

Next you should discuss what you want today in business, but not as individuals, as a partnership or as a team. Decide and agree on your general goals and attitudes to leadership and team performance. Decide these factors and write them down. Post them on the wall and if there's ever an issue, gently – very gently – refer to the loose contract you drew up together when you were both being objective, unemotional and outside the grip of your old leadership blueprints.

Steps for change: Specific experience

STOP (awareness)

Consider a specific emotional incident you experienced in your early life or career that has strikingly affected how you think about managing or leading people. Write down what happened in detail and describe the aftermath.

THINK (understanding)

Now write down how you believe this incident has affected your current leadership style so far.

ANALYSE (break the cycle)

Can you see how your current leadership style may not be helpful to you in managing or leading others? Can you see that it is only what you learned and that it isn't really you? Can you see that you have a choice in the present moment to be different?

START (recondition)

What old ways of behaving can you let go? What new statements can you adopt, what new behaviour can you model to influence a new way of leading? What are you prepared to start believing or doing?

Go to the Seven Failings website at **www.7failings.com** *and go to* **FREE BOOK BONUSES** *to download all our* **'Steps For Change'** *templates*

What is your Leadership Blueprint set for?

What is your Inspirational Leadership Blueprint set for and what results is it subconsciously moving you towards? Are you set for astounding success, for leadership mediocrity or for abject failure? Are you programmed to struggle on as a leader, fighting against all in your path? Or are you able to collaborate with people and – through working hard – create major leadership success for all who surround you? Are you conditioned for a consistent leadership future, where you have the strength to sustain your own, honest, authentic leadership style? Or will there be drastic fluctuations depending on who you are with and what the prevailing climate is in your business?

The point we want to make is that what you actually do from day to day doesn't really matter. What matters is where your leadership blueprint is set and whether you are truly reaching your full leadership potential. Most people tend to believe that the success of their leadership style and even of their business depends mainly on their business skills and knowledge, or at least on their timing in the marketplace. We have a different view. We believe that your leadership success is dependent on your Inspirational Leadership Blueprint, on the extent to which you can mobilise other people round a coherent vision for the future.

Fortunately your personal leadership success can grow. Remember the earlier principle – your leadership success can grow to the extent that you do. So that's what we will continue to do with the rest of this book and even further in the Inspirational Leadership Blueprint Seminar. We will help you to grow.

Remember as you read the rest of this book that the first step on the path is awareness, so watch yourself. Become more conscious of what you're doing and saying. Ask yourself what kind of experiences you are creating for those that follow you.

Importantly you should ask yourself this question: What kind of role model are you?

Most of us like to believe that we live our lives based on choice. But what we've discovered is that there is a surprisingly large number of our actions that are driven by our past conditioning. So if you want to lead in an exciting way, if you want to energise other people to higher levels of performance, you first need to recognise what you're doing poorly so that you can reset your Inspirational Leadership Blueprint.

**Inspirational Leadership
Blueprint Principle**

**Consciousness is observing your thoughts, feelings
and actions so that you can make better choices
here and now rather than be run by the things
you thought or learned in the past**

Once you become a more conscious leader, as opposed to running on autopilot, you can see that your programming in the past is simply a recording of the words and actions you experienced in the past – when you were too young to know any better or decide for yourself what is a better way to lead. You can see that this conditioning is not actually who you are, but who you learned to be. You can see that you are not the recording, but the recorder. You are not the software, but the hardware, capable of rewriting your programming any time you choose.

We have a view that our beliefs are not set in stone, they are simply opinions. Also worth noting is the idea that opinions can be communicated from person to person with more or less certainty. And – significantly – they can cross from generation to generation like the genetic material that makes us up. Knowing this you can consciously choose to release any belief that no longer works for you, or that you no longer want, and move towards success in a different way. Realise that your thoughts and beliefs are not necessarily who you are and that they are not necessarily attached to you permanently.

We said earlier that you shouldn't believe a word we say. Well here's a challenging thought. 'Don't believe a word *you* say. Don't believe a thought *you* think.' Instead, if you want to change your leadership success, study leadership and your leadership style and choose your beliefs and actions wisely. Adopt the thoughts, feelings and actions that are going to lead you to inspire your people to higher levels of performance, productivity and profitability. For that is how successful leaders think and act.

In the next four chapters you'll get a detailed insight into what we call the personal failings of Really Useless Leaders. These are the things that you have total control over. You can improve or develop these at no (financial) cost to anyone. We'll start with the First Failing of Really Useless Leaders. Really Useless Leaders kill explanation.

THE FIRST FAILING

Really Useless Leaders Kill Explanation

How Really Useless Leaders kill productivity by 'mushroom management' and the simple things you can do to use communication to increase business performance

IT WAS A HARD STORY to tell to the interviewer. Mike, a long-time government official, was hunting for words, pausing, thinking aloud. 'The lack of information . . . it definitely makes your job difficult... And if you can't get that self-satisfaction of doing a job, I would think it would be very easy to leave.' Another government worker, Jody, felt the same, though she had only been in the agency a few years. 'The lack of knowledge can become very frustrating and may be disappointing to the point where you don't feel you can achieve any more than what you've achieved... and, therefore, it will affect your wanting to leave.'

These comments – from managers in a large US government agency[3] – are typical of the things people say about 'mushroom management' – the science and art of keeping your people in the dark. And the downside – the impact on morale and retention – is very real.

Now, occasionally managers deliberately keep their people in the dark – perhaps because they feel that the subject under discussion is sensitive. Something like a major relocation or a takeover inevitably brings a degree of secrecy to the proceedings. But sometimes it's just forgetfulness.

Most people we've spoken to have experienced the dreaded executive board 'offsite'. The management team leaves the comfort of HQ for the even greater comfort of an 'offsite' meeting. They're staying at a particularly fancy hotel, occasionally in a different (usually warmer) climate, facilitated by some consultant or business school professor parachuted in for the day. He or she is helping the executive board to analyse all the competitors and to develop a powerful 'knock 'em dead' strategy. After a couple of days of scrawling on flip charts, and the odd round of golf, the senior executive team emerges from the hotel, brandishing pages and pages of notes – their new goals and targets for the business, now miraculously honed into a coherent 'strategy'. (Goals and targets do not a strategy make, but that's a story for another time.)

'That's the strategy,' says the board to their staff. 'Now go for it!' And that's it. No explanation beyond the exhortation to 'Just do it!'. Why don't they explain more of what they want? Why don't they answer the questions their people raise?

Well, many managers seem to assume that:
- everyone 'gets' what our business is about or for
- everyone will 'get' the new strategy easily
- everyone has *already* 'got' it, they're just stalling now
- and everyone will do what we say because we're boss.

It's amazing how quickly managers forget, isn't it? They forget that it took them days of extensive discussion, lobbying and planning to reach their new strategy. But the folks back at the ranch don't have that luxury of time. 'Just do it!' says the boss.

By the way, we're not talking about just a few of the staff who don't understand. Robert Kaplan and David Norton, the Harvard professors who developed the balanced scorecard back in 1996, suggest that only one in five of our people get or understand company strategy as described by senior managers[4]. The important thing to realise, though, is that it isn't that our people are NOT capable of understanding it. The point is that we as the senior executive team don't do a good enough job of explaining the strategy.

And you have probably already experienced what happens next. Yes, the senior executive team is *surprised* that people don't welcome the new strategy with open arms and rush with great enthusiasm to implement it. Because if management realises one thing, it's that if implementation stalls then performance falls.

How 'not explaining' hits your bottom line

Let's consider the direct impact of not explaining. If we take it as read that your new business strategy will deliver greater profitability or reduce your costs, then you need everyone to do things that will deliver greater profitability or greater cost savings. That's a given, right? But if your people just don't understand why you're asking them to go for growth, or why even tougher cost savings matter, then they are unlikely to change what they are already doing. It's incredibly difficult to change the status quo.

And if people won't change what they're doing, you just won't get improved profitability or reduced costs. It won't happen. If this were a game of baseball, that would be strike one.

Here's another reason productivity and profitability get hit – because when you don't explain, your people can't get the information they need to do their jobs properly.

Remember Jody at the start of this chapter? 'The lack of information... it definitely makes your job difficult,' she said. What's the payoff for Jody and people like her? 'If you can't get that self-satisfaction of doing a job, I would think it would be very easy to leave,' she said. So that's the price you pay for forgetting the importance of explaining. And when people leave, you're left with a mess to sort out, new people to find and hire, and inexperienced people to bring up to speed.

But it isn't just the direct impact of not explaining that kills productivity, it's also how our people feel about how we treat them when we don't explain. Let's look at some of the things Really Useless Leaders say when their people ask them to explain.

1) 'It's obvious', 'If you have to ask you don't know' and 'Don't worry your little head about that'.
This mean-spirited point scoring simply programmes people never to ask you for anything ever again.

2) 'The manager's right to manage' and 'Just do as I say'
The know-it-all or control freak's charter simply programmes people to wait to be told what to do.

3) 'You're a stick in the mud' and 'Change is a constant'
Most people are not afraid or unwilling to change. They just need to see the purpose or where a project fits into the overall picture. But phrases like this create a self-fulfilling prophecy. In other words, using this phrase has a tendency to create people who *are* sticks in the mud.

Rudeness and disrespect from managers creates anger, resentment and unwillingness in our people. Strike two for the First Failing of Really Useless Leaders.

But there is more and worse still to come.

How to kill strategic alignment

Perhaps more worrisome still about managers who don't explain is the impact they have on what's become known as alignment – the marrying of people's personal goals with the company goals. If what we really need to do as managers is to get everyone pulling the same way, then we should be explaining the vision and mission of our business in as many different ways as possible. If we can do this, then everyone will pull in the same direction, building on all the activities of the business, creating a business where the whole is greater than the sum of the parts.

In other words, because Pete in engineering knows what the main goal of the business is, he can help Sarah in marketing along the way. And Sarah in marketing can see what else might be helpful for Andrew in human resources. Explaining the overall goals increases the innovation and initiative that exist right across the business.

In essence, then, when we explain what the business vision is, all of our people have a sense of purpose which allows them to add value to everyone's projects. This adds huge value for the business overall. And there's an added benefit. Because if we all know the direction business is heading in, then there is automatically a degree of buy-in or commitment to the goals.

But if we choose NOT to explain, NOT to communicate, then commitment gets undermined in countless little ways, with people chip, chip, chipping away at the strategy and purpose. Not in any way you'd really notice, and definitely not in any way you can easily correct. But the results are dramatic. Having a strategy in the hands of an unaligned workforce is like having a really old car that's getting a little older every day. All the different parts are gradually going wrong and failing, but the car is held together by the layer of rust. You don't know if the car will get through the next service, but there's no one big thing you can fix. There is nothing major that's wrong with it. So strike three is the major impact not explaining has on business alignment.

How to explain

There are dozens of tactics and strategies for communicating with your people, but we'll just cover four of the ones that we use regularly and that we share with our clients in our workshops. They are tactics and strategies that have worked for years so we can recommend them wholeheartedly because they work.

The tactics are these:

■ The reason why
■ 21st century delegation
■ The decision-making continuum
■ The team briefing cascade

1) The reason why

John Patterson founded the National Cash Register company (NCR) in 1884. He was fanatical and autocratic, but he knew one or two things about selling. He trained his sales executives to explain to buyers *why* they needed his machines and he knew how to use explanations to differentiate his more expensive machines from those offered by the competitors.

Patterson also discovered a fascinating side effect of giving his people an arsenal of meaningful sales arguments. Not only did his sales executives sell more products than many others in the industry, they were also more motivated because they knew how to communicate more effectively with their clients. That motivation led to even greater success.[5]

So give your people a clear and simple 'reason why'. Make

sure the reason why is focused on future benefits, and can be answered 'in order to…'. This will be focused on the benefits of the project. If the answer to your reason why is 'because of', it is usually less valuable to you, unless you're explaining why you need to comply with legislation. If you have children you'll recognise that 'do this just because' doesn't work very well.

Another aspect of 'the reason why' is make sure you have answered the question 'what's in it for me' (WIIFM) for your people. They don't want to know the reason why they must comply, they want to know what's in it for them.

**Inspirational Leadership
Blueprint Principle**

Give people a reason why

**And remember that why means 'in order to',
rather than 'just because'**

What makes a good reason why? Give your people technical information showing why this or that equipment is best, fastest, or cheapest and how it will beat the competition hollow. Give them reasons why something will win market share. Give them reasons why we have to move now ('there's a deadline', or 'we'll miss out if we don't do it soon').

Whatever reasons you give people, do give people reasons why. A good reason why becomes a virus that works for you, spreading explanation through the company, even when you're not in the conversation.

In summary, a good reason why does three things:

a) gives a clear purpose

b) can be used to pass on to others

c) buys commitment ('even though I don't agree I can see why they want to...')

2) 21st century delegation

We can use the moment we delegate tasks as a moment to explain why. Here's how it can work. In the diagram below you'll see that there are two people involved. The circle on the left represents you, the manager, and the circle on the right represents your employee, or the team you're delegating to.

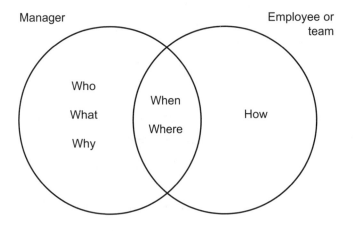

Figure 1: 21st century delegation - who decides what?

In the circle on the left are the things that you the manager should explain, while in the overlap between the two circles are the things you negotiate with the employee or team you're delegating to.

In the circle on the right, however, that's the circle that your employee or your team has responsibility for.

So looking again at the circles, you have responsibility for kickstarting the briefing and basically this boils down to clarifying three things:

1) **who** you want to tackle the project
2) **what** the project is
3) and **why** the topic is important

The circle on the right represents your employee and we'll look at the contents of that circle in a moment.

But in the overlap with your employee you can see two things that need to be negotiated between you. In essence, these are the terms of reference for the project:

4) when will the project be completed
5) where will the project take place

Finally, there's something you should leave entirely to your people to figure out. You should leave them to choose precisely **how** they undertake the project. Your people are smarter than you are when it comes to the nitty gritty of their daily roles. They are best placed to decide how to carry something out.

**Inspirational Leadership
Blueprint Principle**

**Explain why
but let people choose how**

Giving your people this degree of autonomy – the ability to decide how to do something – goes a long way to winning their

commitment and enthusiasm for the project. Spelling out exactly how they should do something, as well as what and why, will
severely reduce their performance on the project. We'll say more
about this in Chapter 4 on the Fourth Failing of Really Useless
Leaders.

3) The decision-making continuum

You know that if you can increase the amount of participation
people have in the decision making process, the more they will be
committed to the decision you jointly reach. Unfortunately some
managers see involving people in the decision making process as
tantamount to giving away their rights to manage. 'Participation
in decision making?' one manager said to us. 'No, thanks – management by consensus never works. It's like communism.'

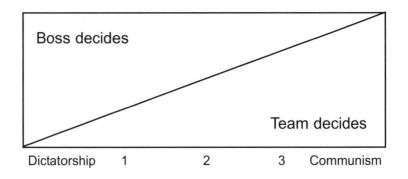

Figure 2: the decision-making continuum - who decides?

But you can see participation in decision making as much
more than black or white, on or off. We suggest you see decision
making as a continuum.

If the box above represents the continuum of decision making, then at the extreme left of the box is the point where you,
the boss, make all the decisions for the team. At the extreme right

is the point where the team makes all the decisions. But in between are a whole host of possible decisions.

About a quarter of the way along from left to right (at point 1 on the box, for example) you might say this:

'Folks, I've pretty much made up my mind on this point, but if you can help me explore some additional possibilities then it will help me make a better decision for the business.'

About halfway along (at point 2) you might say something like this:

'I have some views on how we might do this, but I really need your involvement to explore all the possibilities. I'll work with you and we'll come up with something we all agree works well. But I'll make the final call on this.'

About three quarters of the way from left to right (at point 3) you might say:

'I have no feelings on this one way or the other – I'll support whatever you want to do.'

This almost grants full autonomy to the team, but not quite. And if you don't use the continuum to explain your position, **whenever** you canvass the views of your people they will **always** assume you are giving them total autonomy to decide what to do.

Inspirational Leadership
Blueprint Principle

Invite participation but spell out
who is the decision maker

---

4) The team briefing cascade
Team briefing is a powerful method of cascading information up

and down the levels of any company. It was first developed by the Industrial Society (now the Work Foundation) more than 40 years ago, but probably hasn't been used as extensively as it could be. This is a great shame and is probably because managers are not as skilled in facilitating meetings as they could be.

Now, each briefing includes a mixture of head office and local issues, but the point of the briefing is not so much in the information it cascades, but in how the information is shared. The cascade makes sure, first of all, that staff at all levels receive the information that is relevant to them and that, secondly, they can question senior managers 'at the point of sale', as it were. Now, team briefing is not meant to replace the normal and essential day-to-day communications between managers and their staff, but we believe the process works particularly well because it is **face-to-face**, which is a missing ingredient in all electronic forms of communication.

How the process works is that every month the CEO or the board of directors agree a core brief, covering financial and statistical performance, company policy, business direction and market conditions among other things. But not everything needs to be covered in every briefing. This is then shared in an open face-to-face meeting with the next level of managers.

Now what makes this different from something that could be blasted to everyone by email is that open questions are encouraged and the forum is an opportunity to discuss and explore the elements in the briefing. Then the managers from the board down add their local interpretation and explanation to the core brief before passing the items on to the next level, with the same open questions policy in force.

There are a couple of important points to note. First, the team briefings should be face-to-face. Second, they should take place as soon as possible after the main board's first briefing. Thirdly, the local briefers have a responsibility to present the company line. So to be able to do this sincerely, everyone really needs to understand and explore the issues in each briefing. No one wants to be in the position of saying 'Well, I don't buy this, but I've been told to tell you…'

Finally, team briefing obviously requires a good level of interpersonal skill in reconciling the different priorities of the company with the needs and receptiveness of the teams at each level. But no one said this was going to be easy.

And looking back over the four strategies we've listed here we hope you can see that the common thread running through them is that face-to-face conversation is the key. It is no good trying to introduce major changes, or persuade people to tackle new projects, without face-to-face contact.

**Inspirational Leadership
Blueprint Principle**

**Face-to-face communication
increases productivity,
decreases grievances
and increases retention**

Go to our website **www.7failings.com** and click on the **FREE BONUS DOWNLOADS** section for a list of resources if you want to get started on the team briefing process. This is something we can wholeheartedly recommend as a process – it increases the amount of dialogue and face-to-face conversation across your business.

Conclusion: the benefits of explaining

Really Useless Leaders who don't explain what's going on:

■ increase the likelihood of grievances and disciplinary issues among their staff
■ kill the alignment of personal goals with a company's business mission
■ decrease productivity and morale
■ and lose their best people.

Really Useless Leaders just don't seem to recognize that our people, for various reasons, simply don't understand why we might want something done if we don't explain why. Now, why is this 'why' really important? Well, it turns out that we all need three things from our work. We need to feel that what we're doing contributes to the overall goals of the unit or team. Secondly, we need to know 'why' so that we can refine or even radically improve our job, task or project. Remember our people need to have ownership of 'the how' – if we spell out why we're doing something and our people can come up with a better, faster, cheaper way, then we're all winners.

And finally, all of us need to feel from time to time that we're part of something bigger, a community of collaborating managers. In conclusion, then, a good explanation is worth gold to you. You must constantly give a coherent business case. It motivates people. If nothing else, think of it like a good sales executive regards a good explanation. It can always be passed on to someone else, to help make their job easier.

So as well as setting out what your people need to achieve, you should also explain why, till you're blue in the face and in every medium you possibly can. You must build a workplace where explanation and vision are not buried or skimmed over, but are always open and clear. If it's your job to deliver performance through others, then it's your job to create a clear vision for us all. How good are you at explaining your vision for the business?

And you have to start explaining now

In closing this chapter on the First Failing of Really Useless Leaders let us make a plea. You have to start explaining your vision and strategy *now* and in as many ways as you can. And you have to keep up the momentum. Because explaining takes time. We know this, but sometimes we forget.

Inspirational Leadership
Blueprint Principle

If it's time to get people to do new things –
it's time to make it your mission to explain

If we take it as read that your new business strategy will deliver greater profitability, or reduce your costs, then you need everyone to do things that will deliver greater profitability or greater cost savings. But if your people just don't understand why you're asking them to go for growth, or why even tougher cost savings matter, then they are unlikely to change the status quo. But the inertia of 'the way we do things round here' can't be shifted in a single day. It's the classic situation of the oil tanker heading across the ocean. If you want to change direction, it's going to take you some time. So if you want better performance productivity and profitability from your people, start today.

THE SECOND FAILING

Really Useless Leaders Kill Emotion

Why do toxic managers kill emotion in the workplace? The hard business reasons why emotions should not be stamped out and the simple tactics you can use to help stamp them in

YOU'RE FINISHING A SECOND cup of coffee in the coffee shop when suddenly you tune in to the conversation behind you on the right. 'I dread each day coming to work,' says a voice. You daren't turn round, but you want to. The voice continues. 'Once inside the door I feel chained to my desk like a prisoner. My boss is the prison warder who delights in torturing me with a daily barrage of public criticism and ridicule. I feel so powerless, like a pawn being played in one of his power games. My friends ask me why I just don't quit?... Why do I stay and take that abuse? I don't know why... I guess I hope things will change, even though they don't. So I stay... hating him, and hating myself.'

This story, about a global telecommunications company, is all too common. And while we don't know everything that went on behind the scenes, it's clear that the perceived tyranny has driven this manager to powerless despair.

In many ways this chapter has been the most difficult to write in this book - it's difficult to keep it constructive. It could so easily spiral into a catalogue of recriminations and 'boss from hell' stories. You see, this chapter is about toxic bosses and the Second Failing of Really Useless Leaders, which is this: Really Useless Leaders Kill Emotion in the workplace.

In the pages that follow we want to show you exactly how killing emotion hits the bottom line and exactly what you can do about it.

It may be that you're a manager who is, perhaps, somewhat toxic. But you don't realise it, or the heavy impact that it has on your team. However, in these pages we'll point out the problems toxic leadership creates and suggest ways to overcome these problems.

But before we look at coping or corrective strategies let's first look at the different kinds of toxic boss that exist.

Are you a toxic boss?

Toxic bosses are people who struggle with emotions in the workplace. And though there are many different kinds of toxic boss, the ones who do most damage to the bottom line can be split broadly into the following four categories:

Emotionally Toxic Bosses

1) The 'Tyrant' (an abusive boss)
2) The 'Work is for Work' boss (a blinkered boss)
3) The 'Vulcan' (a logic neurotic)
4) 'Mr' or 'Ms Gravitas' (the great pretender)

Let's deal with these emotionally toxic bosses one at a time and the first and most obvious is the 'tyrant'.

1) The tyrant (an abusive boss)

Some tyrants, no doubt, are well meaning. They are dictatorial and tyrannical 'for the good of the company'. They are trying to train their people to focus on work and are trying to get the best performance out of them. Unfortunately, they often have the opposite effect. Their tyrannical style kills the very thing they want to achieve. Tyrants demotivate managers and actually prevent them from acting as productive members of the firm. They do this in a number of ways.

i) The angry manager

William Watkins, CEO of Seagate Technology, the disk drive maker, is a storm contained only by his skin, says *Forbes* magazine.[6] In 1985, when he was working at a startup called Domain Technology, Watkins got so angry in a meeting that he picked up a chair and threw it at the company president. Watkins wasn't fired, but got a lecture about controlling his temper. 'I've always been too loud, with long hair, always a little too much of everything,' says Watkins. 'I don't inhibit myself.'

But he continued to struggle with his emotions. In 2000 he hurled a cup of hot coffee at a senior executive after the guy publicly insulted the entire notebook division without having all the facts. He apologised for it, but admitted he would do it again.

Now while it has to be OK to get angry at the right time, with the right person for the right reason, that anger needs to be controlled and moderated. It should never spill over into simple abuse or a blatant disrespect for people. Because the danger of the full-on angry manager is that people become afraid to speak out of line or to show any kind of initiative at all. They fear being hauled over the coals in front of everyone else for getting it wrong, or simply for doing something the boss didn't know about or doesn't like. Then there's the fear of being demoted or sidelined for the foreseeable future. And of course there's the fear of being fired on the spot. In other words, the angry manager's impact on the bottom line is to kill action and productivity. Angry managers kill action by intimidating their people. And, yes, even mild sarcasm can be toxic in the wrong hands.

■ Personal Review Questions: Have you ever experienced other people, or yourself, losing your temper uncontrollably? What happened next? What should have happened?

ii) The thoughtless manager

It was THE investment conference of 2003 and Henry Paulson, Jr., chairman and CEO of financial services firm Goldman Sachs was discussing the possibility of future layoffs at the firm. 'I don't want to sound heartless,' he said, 'but in almost every one of our businesses, there are 15 or 20% of the people that really add 80 percent of the value... I think we can cut a fair amount and not get into muscle and still be very well positioned for the upturn.'

Goldman Sachs employees were appalled, interpreting Paulson's comments as a contradiction to the firm's 'we're all in this together' philosophy. 'Internally, it was a real problem,' one high-ranking employee told the *New York Times*. Another said 'People here are very upset. We've always been told that it's about teamwork and not a star system.'

Paulson may have averted a total public relations disaster by apologizing for his off-hand comments right away. Goldman Sachs employees checking their voice messages heard Paulson apologizing for a 'glib and insensitive response' to the question on future layoffs at the company. 'I am profoundly embarrassed about my choice of words,' he said, adding that his comments had 'created an impression completely at odds with my respect for the people who have been let go…Please accept my apologies and gratitude'.

While Paulson was right to try to allay investors' fears about the impact of job cuts on the firm, he perhaps should have considered the personal dimension of what he was saying before he said it.

■ Personal Review Questions: Have you ever experienced other people, or yourself, saying or doing things without thinking: 'Would I like this said about me?' What happened next? What should have happened?

iii) The rude manager

If you want a cast iron example of how managers can immediately and adversely hit shareprice by being rude (as well as angry) consider Neal Patterson. Patterson is still the CEO of Cerner, a US healthcare company, despite wiping 22% off the value of the company's stock with one email, leaked to a Yahoo financial messageboard, in 2001. Patterson then spent three weeks trying to reassure investors that there was no problem. So not only a major hit to the stock, but also a huge waste of senior management time should be added to the bill. (But the damage to morale? Priceless.)

By now you'll want to know what his email to managers read: 'We are getting less than 40 hours of work from a large number of our EMPLOYEES. The parking lot is sparsely used at 8am; likewise at 5pm. As managers, you either do not know what your EMPLOYEES are doing or you do not CARE. In either case, you have a problem and you will fix it or I will replace you.'

And there was more.

'NEVER in my career have I allowed a team which worked

for me to think they had a 40-hour job. I have allowed YOU to create a culture which is permitting this. NO LONGER.' He added that he wanted to see the car park nearly full by 7.30am and half full at weekends. He concluded the email with the chilling words: 'You have two weeks. Tick, tock.'

Once the email appeared on Yahoo, Wall Street analysts started to get calls from anxious shareholders. Stephen Davas of Goldman Sachs said: 'It raised two real questions for investors. Has anything changed at Cerner to cause such a seemingly violent reaction? And is this a chief executive that investors are comfortable with?'

Mr Patterson, who founded Cerner in 1979, attributed his blunt management style to growing up on a farm in Oklahoma. He told the *New York Times*: 'You can take the boy off the farm, but you can't take the farm out of the boy.' Cerner has been included in *Fortune* magazine's list of the 100 best companies to work for in America.

■ Personal Review Questions: Have you ever experienced other people, or yourself, abusing someone without thinking? What happened next? What should have happened?

2) The 'Work is for Work' boss (a blinkered boss)

Not as obviously toxic as the tyrant is the 'work is for work' boss who says things including 'work is for work' and 'leave your personal life at home'. This kind of manager may also belittle small talk and the social side of being at work, thinking it no more than time wasting. But there are limits. In one British company, managers ran a sweepstake to see how long they could go without speaking to the boss. 'It became ridiculous...' reported a manager in the London *Financial Times*. 'The record was made when a colleague and I travelled all the way from Manchester to our London

HQ, including sharing taxis and the British Airways Shuttle, without him ever speaking to either of us! Let's just say his communications problems did not do anything for morale.'

Bosses who do NOT want to know about the interests and passions of their people outside work are missing a huge opportunity to learn what makes them tick. They miss a major source of information about how to motivate people. We'll say more about this in Chapter 5 on pay and reward strategies, but broadly 'work is for work' bosses see no value in really knowing their people, but cost their company hugely in the pocket, by failing to do their jobs as motivators of people.

■ Personal Review Questions: Have you ever experienced other people, or yourself, turning away from knowing your people more closely? Why was this? How could you have improved what happened?

3) The 'Vulcan' (a logic neurotic)

Like Mr Spock, the pointy-eared Vulcan from the science fiction series and film franchise *Star Trek*, the Vulcan boss sees no place for emotions at work and most especially in decision making. According to the Vulcan boss, all business decisions should be made on purely rational, logical grounds. He or she actually devalues emotions as irrational, illogical and unprofessional.

'The last few decades', says writer Daniel Pink in his cult book *A Whole New Mind*, 'have belonged to a certain kind of person with a certain kind of mind.' And he lists them with many different examples early on in the book.

■ computer programmers who can crank out code
■ lawyers who can craft contracts
■ MBA students who can crunch numbers.

This kind of intelligence is what distinguishes us from other animals, says the left-brain Vulcan boss. 'It's our ability to reason analytically - that's what makes us unique.' The Vulcan goes further, demanding that we refuse to pay attention to the touchy feely, weepy and hysterical elements in society which will eventually dumb us down and screw us up.

Not so fast, Mr Spock.

'We are moving from an economy and a society built on the logical, linear, computer-like capabilities of the information age,' says Pink, to an economy and a society built on the inventive, empathetic, big-picture capabilities of what's rising in its place, the Conceptual Age.'

In other words, we need to value both rational, logical thinkers AND the big picture emotional thinkers, he says, and there are senior executives who appear to embody both aspects of leadership. Steven Green, for instance, at HSBC.

Green is now chairman of the global bank, but when he was Chief Executive, he had a potentially tricky issue to deal with in the run up to a public leadership lecture in the UK – 4,000 jobs were being relocated to India and other countries outside the UK and of course it was likely there would be redundancies. The press was having a field day and there was disquiet in the ranks to say the least, which Green acknowledged to the Leadership Trust.

'HSBC seeks to be a decent and fair employer,' he said. 'We work very hard at managing this process of change as sensitively as we can for our colleagues. For instance, in the UK we have set aside £4 million to support and advise staff affected by the changes... But I acknowledge that no matter how sensitively we handle this, it cannot be painless.'

However, he said - and this was the smart sentence that caught our attention - 'if you hide from this issue or pretend it's not there, the reckoning will come later.' Green recognized that the emotional issues associated with the offshoring of thousands of jobs would severely hit morale if nothing was done to support staff going through the change. Other senior executives faced with a similar challenge might simply have said 'Get over it', but Green was able to spearhead an empathetic response that probably prevented a major morale dip at the bank.

■ Personal Review Questions: Have you ever experienced other people, or yourself, devaluing or ignoring the emotional aspects of leading people? Why is this? What more evidence do you need that the emotional aspects of leadership are significant?

4) Mr or Ms Gravitas (the Great Pretenders)

If you're as old as we are, you may remember John McEnroe's famous outburst on centre court at Wimbledon. The young tennis pro petulantly bellowed at the umpire the immortal phrase that will follow him for the rest of his life: 'You cannot be serious!' Well, in business today there are many managers who believe that 'serious' is synonymous with 'professionalism'. Indeed in one global organization we've worked with your perceived 'gravitas' is actually a characteristic that affects whether or not you are considered for promotion. (Seriously.) And there may be more who acknowledge this implicitly when they say things like 'oh, she is definitely one of us'.

This obsession for managers with gravitas – or any other characteristic – creates three difficulties when taken to extremes.

■ *We kill constructive challenge*

We seek to promote people like us, because we're more comfortable with them and there's less conflict, so we create managerial clones and kill differences of opinion – we create a network of cronies, old-school ties and 'yes people'. We don't get honest feedback on our ideas and the chances of getting warnings when things are going pear-shaped are seriously reduced.

■ *We kill playfulness and initiative*

When we look for people with gravitas, we promote people with an exaggerated concern for seriousness, so we kill the climate for playfulness and invention, hampering initiative and productivity.

■ *We worry what others think and kill authenticity*

We behave how we think other people want us to behave, so we kill authenticity and the uniqueness that is us, which is why people will buy our services or work with us in the first place.

People often say to us 'I'm not my real self at work - I'm a different person in the office.' Of course, this is rubbish. They are the same person, they just behave in a different way. They want to be seen to conform, to be in with the in-crowd.

Instead you need to consider Herb Kelleher, chairman and well known former CEO of Southwest Airlines, as he walks down the aisles chatting with customers and handing out peanuts. It's a homely, personable style that fellow airline CEOs have shunned like the plague as an embarrassment. Yet Kelleher has managed to preside over a company that's turned in 31 years of consecutive profit. Do you need a stronger business case for being yourself at work?

■ Personal Review Questions: Have you ever tried to be more serious because you think it's professional? Can you analyse why you think this? What would you do differently if you weren't trying to be more serious? What's the worst that could happen if you behaved in a more authentic way?

Why are 'emotional people' frowned on?

Why are emotional people frowned on? Hasn't there been enough publicity on emotional intelligence to change the way we lead people?

In part, the reason seems related to the belief that fear is a great motivator. Being aggressive can get you what you want. This is certainly true in the short term – coercion and dictatorship can increase performance for a while. But you don't win commitment that way. And today's leaders need both high performance and high commitment from their people.

There's another reason why emotions are shunned by certain managers: they believe that numbers and counting things are the only things that matter in business.

The mantra for these managers is the old phrase 'what gets measured gets done'. While we'd go along with that to a certain degree, though it depends whether what you're measuring actually helps. (Measuring attendance or how long people stay in the office is not the same thing as measuring productivity, for instance.)

Now, many rational managers like to count things and see numbers and measurements as hard quantifiable facts that you can't argue with. But how do you measure the value or importance of human relationships? What about collaboration or co-operation? And then there's concern for customers or employees: how do you measure those? These are things you'd be hard pressed to put a number to. Which explains why many managers see them as unnecessary niceties. Not hard facts that can be managed.

But it is clear that a management style based solely on measurement cannot handle everything that a leader has to take into account. We condemn the assumption that what you can't count doesn't count.

Soon enough people will finally realise that the concept of emotional intelligence has truly broadened our understanding of what it means to be smart. That, in a very real way, emotional intelligence is simply a different way of processing different data. John Meyer, one of the early writers on emotional intelligence, put it this way: 'It means that within some of us who are labelled "romantics", "highly sensitive" or "bleeding hearts", some serious information processing is taking place.'

**Inspirational Leadership
Blueprint Principle**

**Remember that 'emotional' people
process vast amounts of information
in a different way**

How to explore emotion in leadership

If you struggle with what we've covered in this chapter, there are many things that will help you in your leadership style. We've settled here on four connected tactics that we teach and develop in more depth on our workshops. They are tactics to deal with conflict, which is often where the greatest stress is placed on our emotions and our ability to remain on an even keel.

The tactics are these:

- The Story Safari (Walk a mile in my shoes)
- Empathy Experiments (Walk a mile in *their* shoes)
- Building Bridges (Reach out verbally and visually)
- Uncomfortable Conversations (Put the moose on the table)

1) The Story Safari (Walk a mile in my shoes)

The Story Safari is a process of personal reflection, of thinking back over your experience at work – or outside if it's relevant. Set aside 45 minutes or more simply to think back over your time in work. We suggest you do this in chronological order, reviewing and writing down the things you did or said in your past that worked well for you and some of the things that didn't work so well. Note down if you can why you think they worked (or didn't work). Reflect also on the things that other people did or said that had an impact on you.

What interests us in conducting this exercise is that people almost always find that there is an important emotional element in all the examples they choose. Now, managers tend to forget about the early stages of their career, those important moments when they were just formulating their ideas of what leadership is or means to them. So that's why we urge you to think back on your early experiences and to write them down as clearly as you can. Ask yourself these questions:

- What happened?
- Who was there?
- What did everyone say?
- How did this affect any subsequent actions that you took?
- How did this affect the things that you said?

This should take about 45 minutes, but allow as much time as you need to get the full benefit.

What we want you to look for are the helpful and the less helpful things that were said to you and that you in turn did or said to others. After thinking things through you'll begin to realise where your opinions and actions originated and – where necessary – you'll be prodded to tweak your thinking and your action to a more constructive style. We call it a Story Safari because it's as if you're going hunting for those stories or things that happened in your past.

2) Empathy Experiments (Walk a mile in their shoes)

Take all the things you know about someone, an employee, say, that seems very different from you. Imagine in as much detail as you can a particular situation they are in. Now, try to imagine what it's like to be that person. Try to, metaphorically at least, walk a mile in their shoes. What is it like for them in their current role? What is a typical day like for them? Who do they deal with on a regular basis? Who's helpful? Who isn't? How easy or hard is a typical day? What challenges face them? What is REALLY important in this person's life right now?

After exploring what you imagine someone else might be going through, you're much more likely to have an understanding of why they might be behaving the way they do. And having completed these 'thought experiments' you're in a much better position to be able to tackle the next tactic – building bridges.

3) Building Bridges ('Can we talk?')

After you've spent some time imagining what people are thinking or, more importantly, what they're feeling, it's time to reach out and build some bridges with them. There are a number of ways of doing this - if you're skilled in conversation you can always ask how someone feels about an issue. But let's consider a more structured method for getting you from conflict to co-operation.

If there's someone you've been having a particularly hard time with, you need to get them from a position where they're in conflict with you to a place where they may actually co-operate with you. But you need to prepare the ground for a constructive conversation. The structure we recommend takes you both from conflict to co-operation. And how the conversation works in practice is like this:

The Invitation

Invite the person to a short meeting to discuss working methods or working practices. As part of the invitation say something like 'It's important we work together and I'd like to understand your thinking some more.' (Needless to say, you'd better believe this or the other person will spot your insincerity.) Most people usually say yes to the invitation, because they realise the importance of working together.

Step 1: Set the scene on areas of agreement

Ask your partner to summarise areas of work or issues that you both agree on. Agree with them where you can, but don't comment or add to this explanation. Don't take over the discussion. (If you disagree with the assessment, don't comment until later.)

Step 2: Give permission to disagree

Then invite feedback by saying something like: 'I would appreciate hearing the elements of my thinking or the issues that you disagree with.' Do listen, do take notes and do clarify where necessary, but don't debate or defend the issues. It is very important simply to listen through this and probe for more. Ask 'What else is there?'

Step 3: Summarise areas of disagreement

When you're sure there is nothing else to come out, thank them and say 'Now I know there are things we both think are wrong or that we both disagree with. Could you summarise how you see those ...'

Step 4: Ask for permission to disagree with them

Then ask for permission to disagree with the other person. 'Would it be helpful if I summarised or gave you some insights or feedback into which parts of your thinking I have doubts over...?' Most people will say yes, because there is nothing we want more than to know what people think of us. Keep your feedback short and dealing only with the most important or two most important points. Don't make this a litany of problems.

Final summary

After this short feedback session invite your partner to summarise, by going through the steps one more time. 'I would find it helpful if you could summarise where you think we have agreements and where the areas of disagreement are; then perhaps we could look at what we do now...'

It's astonishing to find – after a 15 or 20 minute discussion along these lines – that there's more agreement between you than you realised. And that there is a willingness to explore the remaining disagreements. Or at least to compromise over them in a way that works for you both.

This process of open dialogue works remarkably well. One managing director emailed us the following note after using this approach: 'Since arriving back in Hong Kong I have used the methods in a one-to-one discussion which was always going to be difficult for each of us. I followed the techniques and am convinced the result of the discussion was much better as a result.'

4) Uncomfortable conversations ('Put the moose on the table')

Sydney Taurel, long-time CEO of pharmaceutical giant Eli Lilly, has a great phrase he uses when he wants to explore an uncomfortable conversation. He says 'Let's put the moose on the table.' We wrote about how to do this – with lots of tactics and strate-

---

**Inspirational Leadership
Blueprint Principle**

Don't ignore the obvious

**No matter how uncomfortable it is,
put the moose on the table**

---

gies to help you get started – in *Leadership Unplugged,* the science
and art of strategic conversation. We call them uncomfortable
conversations, because many people sense the conversation will
be uncomfortable and challenging – that is the fear, at least.

We're not alone in promoting this concept, though. We've
worked (too briefly) with Mike Beer at Harvard Business School,
who calls them 'honest conversations', and with Professor Cliff
Bowman, a colleague at Cranfield School of Management, who
calls them conversations in the 'Zone of Uncomfortable
Debate'. Whatever you call them, have them. Put the moose on
the table in a spirit of openness. Much air will be cleared.

'No assholes!'

Really Useless Leaders who kill emotion are widespread. So if
any part of this chapter sounds like it might be a little close to
home for you then we're not surprised. Kevin Kennedy, CEO of
US components giant JDSU, formerly a close colleague of John
Chambers at Cisco Systems, puts it this way: 'What about the person who is emotionally disconnected? For those employees of
yours who feel disenfranchised the first thing that you've got to
do is look critically at yourself and see what it is that's created this
situation. It involves the leader as well as the individual. In fact,

often the leader is the problem."[9]

So we urge you to reflect on the impact you're having on the people round you. Productivity and performance will improve if you can find out more about what motivates your people and if you can learn to use different emotional levers – levers other than coercion and fear.

Inspirational Leadership
Blueprint Principle

Civilised workplaces are not a naive pipedream –
adopt a zero-tolerance attitude to 'assholes'

We also know that creating a positive workplace has a dramatic and positive effect on how persistent people are in making things work. Killing emotion in the workplace stops people trying so hard to do their jobs.

We haven't gone into here the new science of 'happiness' and the idea that happy people are productive people, but let's just say there's more to being a supportive, empathetic leader, than just being 'touchy feely', 'fluffy' or 'nice'. There is a hard business reason for NOT killing emotion.

We leave you with the thought captured in Bob Sutton's recent book *The No Asshole Rule*[10] 'As soon as people heard the title,' he said, 'they started telling me great stories, pointing me to sources and doing a host of other favours for me that made it the most delightful and energising writing adventure of my life.' In some ways it's a shame Bob's best work is focused on assholes.

In the next chapter we'll look at how Really Useless Leaders kill engagement.

THE THIRD FAILING

Really Useless Leaders
Kill Engagement

What do you have to STOP doing right away
if you want to get your people working together
for the good of the company and performing at their peak?

WHY IS EVERYONE TALKING about employee engagement? Unless you've been hiking in Nepal you can't have missed that everyone from Jack and Suzy Welch down is ranting about the importance of employee engagement. Global corporations including HSBC and Microsoft are running surveys on employee engagement annually, if not monthly, and the virtual shelves at Amazon are groaning under the weight of countless new books on the subject. But cynics still wonder 'Is it really that big an issue?'

Yes, says market research giant Gallup. Gallup's research, based on interviews with thousands of employees worldwide, reveals that most workers are not engaged in – or are actively disengaged from – their work. In the US in 2006, about 56% were not engaged, says Gallup, 15% were actively disengaged and only 25% were actively engaged. Now, these numbers might seem big, but hold on. How much does disengagement matter financially?

Well, says Gallup, in the second quarter of 2006 in the US, the actively disengaged workforce – that's people undermining the goals of the business and actively destroying value – cost the economy about $328 billion. (For more details on these statistics check out the website and the full data at gallup.com.)

And this isn't just a US phenomenon. The picture is repeated in Gallup's surveys all around the world, as well as in surveys from other institutions. In the UK, research company Hay reports that employees would be as much as 45% more productive if they were 'doing a job they were really engaged with'. And a 45% increase in employee productivity would be worth up to £340bn added output per year to the UK service sector alone. So engagement *is* a big issue if you want to boost performance and profitability.

OK, pollsters, let's assume you've got numbers to back up your argument that engagement matters. But if engagement *was* such a big issue, you'd expect the world's leaders and managers to be doing something serious about it, wouldn't you? They're not.

'While our bosses pay lip service to "employee engagement" and "our people are our best asset" all they really do is *tell* us to be more engaged," says Marco, during a coffee break at a workshop in Rome. Marco is a regional manager in an international real estate company. 'But you can't just *tell* people to be more engaged. You have to build a company where we can *be* more engaged. Right here, in this company, that is not the case at the moment.'

A colleague from Eastern Europe, Sonja, nodded vehemently. 'That is right. And while the executive board has done a lot of things to be thankful for, they cannot seem to talk the language that my team and my office workers understand. They talk on and on about the share price and about creating value for the shareholders. For my deputy Anja this is not why she comes to work. There is a huge gap with the board.'

Conversations like this one, with managers in dozens of firms, in many different industries, suggest that Really Useless Leaders are using the same two approaches to win the hearts and minds of their people:

1) They try a well meaning but misplaced dictatorship as they 'demand' engagement from their employees;
2) and they have an understandable but equally misplaced obsession with shareholder returns as the main thing that people should be engaged with.

Both approaches are understandable and extremely well meaning, but wholly wrong. This is the Third Failing of Really Useless Leaders. They kill engagement.

**Inspirational Leadership
Blueprint Principle**

**You can't just tell people to be more engaged –
You have to stop disengaging them**

Engagement is a joint commitment

If you're married, you probably remember the day you got engaged to your partner. You may have imagined that everything would be just marvellous and a never-ending sequence of complete happiness. Perhaps you were more pragmatic, realising that there would be ups and downs. But you almost certainly knew that it would be a two-way commitment. That's what an engagement between people is meant to be – an open-ended, two-way commitment between equals.

Of course, engagement between boss and employee isn't quite like this in business – but we suggest that the idea of engagement as a two-way commitment is worth exploring. We very much like the idea that managers and employees should support one another in a mutual or dual accountability.

But put that to one side for a moment, because there is a more important point to address right now – the forgotten key that will unlock the engagement puzzle for many leaders.

Engagement with what?

When we talk about employee engagement we don't usually mean the engagement of employees with a leader or with the whole executive board. We mean the engagement of employees with something else. But what exactly? If we can understand this, then we have the key to unlocking the whole question of engagement and how to build a workforce that is truly engaged.

Alison Portlock sits at the centre of the International Innovation Network, a global web of accountants and finance directors from Europe, the US and Asia-Pacific. She describes her leadership style as facilitative and collaborative. 'I really believe that we need to get the best out of people and teams and that that's the purpose of a leader.' But she is equally certain that the company does not exist for its people. 'The purpose of business is not to provide a living for its employees,' she says. Portlock is in absolutely no doubt that the purpose of the corporation should be focused entirely on creating shareholder returns for its investors. 'It's the Chartered Accountant in me,' she says.

And every professor of accounting and finance will agree,

arguing that this the only thing enshrined in a company's articles of association. 'A company's sole legal purpose is to grow, make a profit and return the profits to the shareholders,' they'll say. 'And you can't argue with the law can you?'

No. But you also can't argue with the fact that creating profits to give back to the shareholders doesn't really get most people leaping out of bed in the morning.

'Get over it and knuckle down,' say the accountants. 'Engage with the purpose of the company.'

'No, and go hang,' say the 21st century's increasingly voluble employees, who go slow and do just enough to get by without actually getting fired.

A stalemate.

Or is it?

We'd like to suggest that it's all a terrible misunderstanding and that it can be cleared up in just a few minutes.

What gets you out of bed in the mornings?

If you're a CEO you're absolutely paranoid about the shareprice of your firm. Your salary depends on it. Your bonus depends on it. Your job depends on it. Like many other companies, hospitality company Whitbread posts a flashing red up-to-the-minute tickertape of the shareprice in its main lobby. 'I wanted everyone to see the shareprice and to see it changing,' says Alan Parker, Whitbread CEO. 'We put it right there in the lobby so everyone could see it and feel connected to it.'

Parker is right to be concerned about share price. And so is the executive board. Their salaries and bonuses, and to some extent their jobs, are also dependent on the shareprice. And as the executive board, their professional purpose is to act as stewards for the shareholders of the firm. For them shareprice is everything. For this is the purpose of the executive board. They are professional servants of this vehicle we call 'the corporation'.

But many of the other professionals in the business will not share that goal. Engineers, marketers and human resource professionals, for instance, usually don't get out of bed in the morning for the shareholders. Neither do the clerical workers, shop floor workers and canteen staff.

Of course, they do in reality. Their salaries depend on shareholders getting quarterly returns, their jobs depend on it, their careers depend on it. But ask folks individually what motivates them to work and they'll give you quite a different answer.

Take teachers. Governments hire teachers to educate the workforce of tomorrow, to create a more competitive economy for the country as a whole. But is that why any individual teacher teaches? Zoe, who teaches accounting to teenagers, says 'I suppose it's in there somewhere, it's in the intellectual mix of teaching, but the over-riding satisfaction of teaching for me is seeing someone "get it". Seeing someone do something they hadn't been able to do before. When they see double-entry book-keeping for the first time, for instance, and it seems like magic... when both the columns add up – that's what teaching is about.'

Kathy Sierra has been a computer game developer for people including Virgin and MGM, and is co-creator of a publishing company for techies. She writes an astonishing blog called 'Creating Passionate Users'. It should be required reading for everyone in management, let alone anyone trying to engage their users. And on this topic of engagement, she is adamant.

'People ask me, "How can I get our employees to be passionate about the company?" Wrong question,' she says. 'Passion for our employer, manager, current job? Irrelevant. Passion for our profession and the kind of work we do? Crucial.'

The company, she says, should 'support people in doing what they're trying to do, and stay the hell out of their way... The best company is one in which the employees are so engaged *in their work* that the company fades into the background.'

And this is the secret of engagement. Employees shouldn't be sleeping in their cubicles to prove they're 'passionate' employees. 'The happiest moments of my work life,' says Sierra, 'were on projects where we pulled all-nighters because we wanted to, not because the corporate culture said we weren't a true team-player/trooper if we didn't.'

So at the level of the professional manager, engagement is with the profession, whether that means the programming profession, design, engineering, animation, science, publishing, education, architecture or entertainment. Engagement also occurs at the level of the people who pull it all together, the producers and assistants who support the professionals and make things happen.

Money or financial returns then become an outcome of successfully doing something that people want to do well. Money – whether profit or cost saving – is simply the way we keep score of the value that's been exchanged.

How to be profitable? Don't look for profit

This, of course, is a profit-seeking paradox. 'We want profit, but we shouldn't look for it? Wha...?' Well, ask yourself this: why is it that some of the most profitable companies in the world are not the most profit-oriented?

In their 2002 book, *Built to Last: Successful Habits of Visionary Companies*, Jim Collins and Jerry Porras compared outstanding companies with adequate but less remarkable companies with similar operations. Merck and Pfizer was one of the comparisons they made and Collins and Porras compared the philosophy of George Merck with that of John McKeen of Pfizer.

George Merck	John McKeen, Pfizer
'We try never to forget that medicine is for the people. It is not for the profits. The profits follow, and if we have remembered that, they have never failed to appear. The better we have remembered it, the larger they have been'	'So far as humanly possible, we aim to get profit out of everything we do'

Figure 3: clear company profits follow clear business purpose

Collins and Porras also compared Hewlett-Packard with Texas Instruments, Procter & Gamble with Colgate, Marriott with Howard Johnson, and found the same result in each case. The company that put more emphasis on profit in its declaration of objectives was the less profitable in its financial statements.

An interesting aside on this point highlights the uneasy tension between shareholder value and business success. Henry Ford was sued by shareholders who resented his determination to expand his automotive business rather than distribute the profits. When they won their case, most of the dividend that the court required the Ford Motor Company to pay went to Ford himself. He then used the money to buy back stock and regain his freedom of operations. For much the same reasons, Sir Andrew Lloyd Webber took The Really Useful Group, the production company responsible for global blockbusters including

'Cats' and 'Phantom of the Opera', back into private ownership in 1991 after only five years trading publicly. (In both cases, dissatisfied stockholders would probably have done better to keep quiet.)

So while we say 'Yes, the purpose of a company is to return money to its shareholders', we'll also say 'the purpose of a business is to do business'. In other words, it is the collection of professionals, all working together at their peak, that will deliver the returns the shareholders want. And that means a different leadership role for the executive board than the 'plan, direct and control' role that they would otherwise take.

How can leaders engage their people?

If the role of the board is not to *tell* people to be engaged, but just to get out of the way, then the role of the board becomes elevated to a much higher, more strategic level. Like the character Morpheus played by Laurence Fishburne in *The Matrix*, a classic leadership movie, leaders should be finding the best people, training the heck out of them and letting them get on with the job. Leaders should be talent scouts, talent developers and role models. They should be designing brilliantly flexible organisations, and finding the best people to fill every role, helping them to specialise as necessary. Only by helping people to specialise in different areas will senior executives help the company to fulfill its goal. And none of this involves the employees pledging allegiance to the corporation.

Far more than it ever was in the past, the role of the leader becomes abundantly clear: it is to help the different parts of the company to increase their value to the business, to become the best creators of value in whatever they do, whether that's engineering, marketing, operations, human resources or even accounting. If senior managers took this approach more often then employees would value the support and would be more engaged and more productive, creating more profit as a natural outcome of being engaged with their professional business purpose. This engagement – of enlightened boss with enlightened employee – IS that joint commitment of equals that we talked about earlier.

**Inspirational Leadership
Blueprint Principle**

**Creating shareholder value is the
purpose of the company**

**But the purpose of the business
is what drives managers and employees**

When new employees start at WL Gore & Associates, the maker of Gore-Tex fabrics, they often refuse to believe that the company doesn't have a hierarchy with job titles and bosses. It just doesn't fit their expectation, their frame of reference. It usually takes several months for new hires to begin to understand Gore's reframed idea of what makes a productive workplace and how the company relies on self-directed employees making their own choices about what to work on and working together in small, highly collaborative teams.

Gore is a success because it seems to be able to get people to exchange one frame for another. It is tough enough when you're working one-on-one, but it's very hard to do with large groups of people, especially if all your previous leadership experience has been 'command and control'. But right now let's summarise the key tactics and strategies that will help you to stop killing engagement in the workplace and at the same time boost performance and – yes – shareholder returns.

How to stop killing engagement

There are some things you need to stop doing and some things you need to change if you want to engage your people systematically in generating greater performance, productivity and profitability. As an important by-product these four steps will give you, the leader, more time to focus on the strategic level issues that you're really paid to focus on.

1) STOP banging on about shareholder value to the WRONG people. The mantra of 'shareholder value' only motivates board level executives.

2) BECOME BILINGUAL. Change the language you use with managers and professionals below board level. Talk about BUSINESS PURPOSE and PROFESSIONAL PURPOSE (If you have to talk about shareholder value, point out that if they do their job well that will lead naturally to shareholder value. Just don't make it their job to create shareholder value.)

3) Third, STOP setting SOFT targets for your teams – allow teams to set their own targets and goals (under the guidance of a local manager). You'll be surprised how much people set stretch goals for themselves and their teams. (More on this in a moment.)

4) Fourth, BUST the silo mentality, or at least BUILD LINKS between the silos. Once you've got your interfering self out of the way, you have more time to make sure everyone's working

together. Break down departmental silos and creating interacting work teams that network with each other for mutual benefit. .

Now, let's look at each of these in a little more detail.

1) Stop banging on about shareholder value to the wrong people

You recognise that shareholder value is important, crucial even, but it doesn't engage most professionals, or those below the board who don't (or don't yet) aspire to board-level. Remember that shareholder value is a purpose of the corporation, but it isn't the business purpose.

Sometimes you need a way of getting this straight in your own mind, so just ask yourself which came first, the business or the corporation? The long and the short of it is: please stop banging on about shareholder value to the wrong people.

2) Become bilingual: talk 'shareholder value' with the board and 'business purpose' with managers below that

Stop talking in the language of the corporation to people who only care about their profession. Use the language of the professionals: describe your business purpose, your vision, in terms that will motivate professionals. Show them where they fit into the big picture.

Analyse the different professional audiences in your company according to these three things:
a) who are you dealing with?
b) what specifically do they do?
c) and why do they do it?

Then your leadership role becomes simple: help them to fulfil their professional role as best they can. Help them to fulfil their professional potential.

3) Allow teams to set their own stretch targets

One of the things we really do know from studies over more than 50 years is that people set stiffer goals for themselves than their bosses can And we know that people are more committed to achieving goals they've had a hand in setting. So if you want better performance from people, the answer is simple. Give them the big picture – what is it you're trying to achieve in broad terms? – let them set their own goals and give them the resources to get going. Why does this work?

Gary Latham, at the Rotman School of Management in Toronto, has been studying this aspect of leadership for 40 years – he literally wrote the textbook on goal setting and motivation. And he believes the success of letting people set their own goals can be explained by two things: first, that setting specific and challenging goals gives purpose, challenge and meaning to what would otherwise become tedious and physically or mentally repetitive. Secondly, he believes that there is huge psychological benefit to setting your own goals and targets.

■ It allows you to focus on what you think is important
■ If it's challenging it energizes you and you're likely to work harder to achieve the goal.
■ Because it's tough you're going to have to work harder for longer – you'll have to be persistent.
■ And because it's important to you, you'll have to learn for yourself how to overcome any hurdles you stumble across. You'll be inspired to find new ways of solving your problems, to innovate or demonstrate initiative.

All of these are things that a firm's leaders must have at the top of their agenda. But if leaders understand that letting people set their own goals increases performance, why doesn't it happen more often? Why have we included it as part of the Third Failing of Really Useless Leaders?

A dispute between the four R&D directors at the Weyerhaeuser Company, a US forest products company, high-lights the challenge[7]. They were trying to figure out what would motivate highly educated employees to become even better at what they do.

One director suggested just setting the goals and targets for the managers. 'After all, that's what happens to us.' The second director, an avid reader of management books and journals, advocated participatively setting goals. Still another believed that goal setting was only appropriate for lower level employees, such as loggers. Scientists and engineers were already highly goal ori-ented, he said. A financial bonus scheme was the answer here, he concluded. The fourth director stress the need for public recog-nition within the company rather than a bonus.

Bets were raised and – being researchers – experiments were set up. Some teams were offered financial bonuses, while some were formally recognized. Some were consulted over goals while another team was just kept in the dark.

The results? Participation increased performance every time. First, because the teams participating in goal setting set stiffer goals (and achieved them). Secondly, because the tasks of the groups were more complex than logging, the team's problem solving knowledge was needed. And with their participation, the team members were able to make sure that relevant and practical solutions could be found. Over 500 studies across industries, cul-tures and age groups have shown that participation works.

'But I've tried that – it doesn't work'
Some managers we've spoken to report that they have tried par-

ticipation in goal setting, but that workers always seem to take the soft option, setting easy goals. When leaders say this we always ask two questions:

1) 'How long did you try for?'
2) 'How much support did you give the team?'

Sometimes we've found it's a particular challenge for the boss to make this happen. In other circumstances, the team has been challenged to make it work.

Alicia's experience in her previous company is fairly typical. 'The last boss I had reminded me of my dad teaching me to ride a bike,' she said. 'He was always there, just over my shoulder, ready to grab the handlebars. And he would *always* grab the handlebars, even when I was perfectly all right. He was more frightened than me.' So bosses do have to give this a fair chance.

For the employees, with any change in working practices there will always be hesitancy and uncertainty. 'How does this work?' 'What does the boss really want?' 'Is this some kind of test?' 'When will things go back to the old way?'

If you've experienced this challenge with teams you might try putting yourself in their shoes for a moment. Ask yourself why might folks set soft targets?

The answers are, of course, that they feel isolated, unsupported or threatened. R&D feels isolated because 'we're going to lose out in the battle with marketing'. Marketing feels isolated because 'the boss always sides with R&D'. The truth is somewhere in the middle. But if you have no inter-team relations there will always be a silo mentality, hurting productivity and performance dramatically.

If a team feels unsupported, with no sign of people, time or resources to tackle a project – guess what? They build in slack. No wonder you think they've set easy goals.

If a team feels threatened or exposed working in a new way, they'll take things real slow, moving forwards just an inch at a time. Why? So they can scuttle back to safety at the first sign of trouble.

Another bike story comes to mind – this time it's our son Christopher, who in the early stages of learning to ride, is wobbling all over the place. Dad twitches nervously 'Shall I...? Shan't I grab the handlebars?' Eventually Christopher yells in exasperation 'I'm wobbling because I'm waiting for you to grab the handlebars. Leave me alone!'

The key to the puzzle: inter-teambuilding

What needs to be in place to make team goal-setting really work? Well, of course, there needs to be a clear vision for the business and meaningful freedom actually to set their own goals. Clear incentives to tackle goal-setting are helpful, clear rewards, though not necessarily financial. (More on this in Chapter 5.)

But above all teams need to know, or need to get to know, the other teams they'll be depending on. And this has to happen at two levels. First at the senior management level.

When the International Downstream Division of Conoco Phillips wanted to take its Billion Dollar Strategy worldwide, VP for the Downstream business Greg Goff had no doubts what to do. 'Let's get folks together and explore the issues with them. Show them what we're looking for, then let them take it down to the next level.' All 70 of Goff's senior management team spent two days at La Manga in Spain to really get to grips with the overall vision for the business – generating a billion dollars' worth of value for the business: 60% above the line in new territories and new deals, 40% from cost savings and efficiencies.

Steven was there facilitating some of the strategy discussions, getting different managers working together to increase the likelihood that they would be able to rely on each other when push came to shove.

At the next level down you need to have the members of each of the management units also working together, so that the head of marketing and the head of engineering, the head of sales and the finance manager know each other and can see that they are one team, working together for the good of the company.

Ludo de Bock is Microsoft's manager for Global Strategic Accounts in Brussels. His team works with major clients including NATO and the European Union. And for two days one summer we worked together to share our thoughts on the challenges of leadership and of interteam working, but also to do about half a day of business planning together.

At the end of the second day, Tony Pellerin, Defence Solutions Manager, turned to Ludo, saying 'You're really ahead of the curve here, Ludo.' His face was a picture of mild disbelief. 'Like many firms we're sometimes poor at planning ahead. We normally do it in August and by September we've normally figured out where we're going. But here you are on the first of June and you've got your plan almost in place.' Ludo smiled and said: 'It's all down to you guys. You learned more about each other over the last two days than we have in a long time. You know that you can rely on Andreas and Zdinek knows he can rely on Marco. Now we just have to deliver.'

So the final piece of the jigsaw, the key to engagement, is to build interacting teams. Ensure the board talks about shareholder value only with the board and with investors. The board should also work with senior managers just below board level to create a management group that can rely on each other – this reduces the fear of isolation and threat.

Then these managers have to take the message to their teams, and guide them through the goal setting process, too. If the cascade works well the performance and productivity of the business in the frontline will generate outstanding shareholder returns as the different arms of the business function better than ever together, for the good of the business and the shareholders.

Really Useless Leader ask the question 'Why are my people not engaged with the business?' But that's the wrong question. A better question is 'why haven't I engaged my people and what can I do about it?'

THE FOURTH FAILING

Really Useless Leaders Kill Enthusiasm

How to inspire your people to higher levels of performance,
productivity and profitability without lifting a finger

KIMBERLY LIVES AND WORKS on a ranch under the clear blue New Mexico sky. The pace of life is slow and every day she rides her young stallion, Toby, a giant black Percheron. Around the pen, she rides, across the desert or splashing through the arroyos, newly carved through the badlands by the sudden torrential rain. Although Kimberly is as far as you can be from the concrete cubicles of city life, she knows everything there is to know about micromanagement – the curse of the control freak.

'In the equestrian world, micromanaging a horse is a sign of the inexperienced or even the incompetent,' she says. A control freak jerks constantly on the reins, kicks hard with her heels, and has equestrian skills that are unrefined and basic. Frankly, says Kimberly, telling a horse exactly where to put its hooves and when shows one thing only: that the rider is actually afraid of the

1,000 pound beast, which is seen more as a threat than a partner. Trust is also missing from the relationship. But her main conclusion when she sees a control freak is this: 'Fundamentally, the micromanaging rider lacks confidence in his own horsemanship.'

But control is a good thing, isn't it? Where's the harm in it? 'Often,' says Kimberly, 'the immediate responses you see in a horse who is being micromanaged are pinned ears (a sign of being angry) and a wringing tail (more anger, and frustration, too). Micromanaging the horse is the ideal way to make him numb, to the point where he'll simply tune you out.'

Micromanagement in the workplace is also the result of inexperience, though it can be the result of incompetence, too. It certainly shows a lack of finesse. And as with the micromanaging horseman or woman, it seems to be driven by fear. Fear of losing control. Fear of letting go. Fear of being shown up. Fear of being perceived as less knowledgeable. So to make up for the fear, the control freak has to know everything, sanction everything, 'lead' everything.

Whatever the root cause of micromanagement, it is astoundingly common and is one of the most hateful things a manager can do to his or her subordinates. A *Fast Company* survey in 2004[13] ranked micromanagement as the third most appalling characteristic of 'jerk bosses'. You might think that doesn't sound so bad, except that the second most appalling characteristic was 'lying' and the most heinous was 'belittling people'. Micromanagement is a big deal.

And yet if you asked a thousand managers to describe their management style very few would see themselves in that light.

Why is micromanagement so bad? Well, it removes freedom of action and autonomy, which is increasingly in demand today from smart managers. Micromanagement prevents employees from using their brains, their training and their experience. It stifles innovation, initiative and experimentation. It undermines any feelings of effectiveness, satisfaction and pride in your work, along with any intention of using your brain at work.

'To get anything done round here, you ask permission,' says Ian, a manager of an engineering division for a global telecommunications company. 'Our new boss has created a permission culture. You can't breathe without he has to know.'

A horse whisperer such as Monty Roberts would say 'The more you use your reins, the less they'll use their brains.' In short, micromanagement removes any enthusiasm an employee might have for their role. And this is the Fourth Failing of Really Useless Leaders: Really Useless Leaders Kill Enthusiasm.

What's the problem with micromanagement?

Dave worked for a large manufacturing company in southern USA for about twenty years. He had a series of promotions over the years and when Robert Hurley at Fordham University in New York met him he was a Vice President with about 3,000 people working in his part of the business.[12] 'Dave had many strong management qualities,' says Hurley. 'He was smart, knew the business well, was very organized, extremely detail-oriented and was regarded as a man of high integrity and ethics. He was also good at assigning tasks and following-up. He seemed to have a very good handle on his operation.'

But when Hurley began working with Dave he noticed some problems with leadership style. 'When we talked to Dave's subordinates they felt that he didn't give them much running room.' They felt that Dave's need to know everything was slowing decisions and creating lots of extra work for people. Dave's direct reports did not feel challenged by what they saw as needless administration and were frustrated that he tended to want things done in particular ways that closed off their creative thinking.

More importantly, because of the way Dave ran his unit, he created a rod for his own back. Some of the people who reported to Dave's managers expressed frustration at having to deal with anyone except Dave. 'If Dave is going to make all the decisions, why am I talking to my manager who has no authority? I want to talk to the decision maker.' Dave's controlling behavior was undermining the credibility of his direct reports, all of whom were talented managers. And he was paying the price by having to deal with things that his managers should have dealt with.

The cost of micromanagement and the impact that Dave's behaviour had on people and the organisation was summed up neatly by Rhonda: 'I don't think he saw himself this way, but his style of leadership devalued the people around him. We never really felt like he trusted us. The end result was that the whole management structure worked just to give him what he wanted. Nobody really "owned" anything because he had his fingers in everything. All authority flowed through him. As a result, there was little or no creativity and no one felt empowered or fulfilled.'

In the end, Dave's performance suffered because he was not challenging people with stretch goals, nor was he empowering people and holding them accountable. He was too involved in tightly controlling his managers and was not spending time clarifying strategy, shaping a high-performance culture and making sure he had the right people to execute the strategy. Dave was eventually moved into a less responsible position during a major corporate reorganisation.

Dave is just one example of an executive whose excessive need to control events, things and people, to get everything perfect and to avoid mistakes, just got in the way of his becoming an inspirational leader. Many successful executives could be described as intense, driven, or success-oriented people. They are intent on achieving goals, sometimes even obsessed with achievement. But Robert Hurley makes an important distinction: there's a difference between the 'healthy' perfectionist and the unhealthy or 'apprehensive' perfectionist. For the apprehensive perfectionist, the source of their drive is not a desire to excel, but the fear of making mistakes, being seen as incompetent, or simply not performing up to their own or others' expectations. And while fear of failure is motivating to a certain degree, it also has undesirable side effects. It stops you enthusing and inspiring people and – as Dave found – it can hold you back in your career.

There are other, hidden costs, too. In today's business environment, where good people are hard to come by and where they know their own worth, they will leave a micromanaging manager. Today the employee is less of a resource for the company and more like a mobile investor of his or her own human capital.

There's more than just anecdotal evidence that micromanagement is a problem. In 2005 the Leadership Forecast study by DDI, a global consulting firm specialising in leadership research of this kind, surveyed more than 1,500 leaders and more than 1,400 associates from 14 countries around the world. Their survey indicated that more than two thirds of leaders were overly concrete in specifying tasks and were far too micromanaging. We conclude that micromanagement is common and if the outcome of micromangement is the death of enthusiasm, you face an uphill struggle as a leader. What's the alternative?

Teach people to think

American actor Kevin Spacey seems to have cornered the market in psychotic guys. From *The Usual Suspects* to *Seven,* Spacey captures the imagination with larger than life human monsters. One black comedy you might have missed, however, is a gem for a leadership professor's class. In *Swimming with Sharks* Spacey plays Buddy, a Hollywood film producer who demands his latest gopher fetch him a coffee – with a sachet of Sweet'n'Low. When the gopher brings the wrong sweetener, Buddy explodes. 'Do me a f'n favour. Shut up, listen and learn. I know this is your first day and you don't really know how things work around here so I will tell you. You – Have – No – Brain! No judgement calls are necessary. What you 'think' means nothing. What you 'feel' means nothing. You are here for me. You are here to protect my interests and to serve my needs. So while it may look like a little thing to you, when I ask for a packet of Sweet'n'Low – that's what I want. And it is your responsibility to see that I get what I want. Am I clear?'

Kathy Sierra, self-styled Chief Poohbah at Head First Books, takes a different view of leadership. 'If you asked 100 managers which they'd prefer – employees who think, or mindless zombies who respond only (and exactly) as ordered, you'd get 100 responses of, "What a ridiculous question. We hire smart people and stay out of their way so they can do their jobs." And if you asked 100 managers to define their management style, none

---

**Inspirational Leadership
Blueprint Principle**

**Hire smart people and stay out of their way –
Don't create zombies at work**

would claim to be micromanagers. Probe deeper, though, and the truth begins to emerge.'

Of course, micromanagers don't actually create zombies, says Sierra, they just inspire zombie-ism on the job. 'Follow those zombies home, and their zombiness vanishes. Their eyes light up, their brain kicks in, and their passion for playing with their kids, championing a cause, or just playing their favourite after-work hobby emerges. You see the side of them that micromanagement crushes.'

Jean Hill is Executive Director of Infrastructure for the Retail Division at Morgan Stanley and she agrees that micromanagement kills the need for people to think for themselves. And her belief that fighting micromanagement is so important has evolved, she says, from her experience as a parent.[23]

'I am teaching my kids how to think. So I give them the thought process behind my decisions, but I am really teaching them how to survive on their own. All too often in the workplace a manager focuses on getting the job done. They just tell the person what to do. And they do not teach them how to think. And they do not teach them what are the critical decision factors.'

OK, let's play devil's advocate for a second. If micromanagement does stop some people thinking, so what? You don't want everyone thinking at work do you? You want some people actually just doing what the boss tells them, right? So is all this really important or is it just a storm in a teacup? What other effect, if any, does micromanagement really have?'

Well, says Hill, apart from the devastating direct impact on employees and subordinates, micromanagers can actually hinder **their own** career progression.

'I think for managers to make it to the next level is really about cultivation [of talent] and about who's on the bench. And about getting people to be better than you. And really, really about teaching them. That is where I spend probably more of my time.' And it's not easy. 'Giving them too much rope so that they can hang themselves is just as bad as micromanaging them and telling them what to do.' You have to figure out how to let go and how far to let go for yourself.

'Get real,' says pro-micromanagement lobby

So are all micromanagers clueless or evil? Of course not. Most of them just suffer from a misguided belief that there isn't enough time to get people to do the job properly (ie their way) or up to the right standard (ie their standard).

This is a myth, in our opinion, but it's prevalent in the fast-moving, fast-paced business world. Especially if you have a logical left brain like Ed Borasky.

Borasky is a Linux programmer and mathematician who agrees that micromanagement isn't helpful, but he – metaphorically, at least – shrugs his shoulders. What can you do?

'You can blog about how you have a "better" way, you can drop out, and still the fact remains – well over 90% of us function in an accountability hierarchy... And while we all know that business is about people first, and money, time, goods and services second, an accountability hierarchy is about money and time.'

Those two words 'accountability' and 'hierarchy' are important, says Borasky, because people *are* accountable for their actions and their business results. And the structure *is* hierarchical, so: 'Your boss is accountable to his or her boss for what you and your teammates say and do.'

We're not arguing with this, only that 'how' you tackle the question of performance, productivity and profitability is not solved by micromanagement. Is a CEO accountable for the business results of her managers? Yes. Is the CEO therefore obliged to micromanage her managers? No. Surely the answer is to hire and develop great managers and get out of their way?

Enough on micromanagement itself, let's look at tactics of turning around the unenthusiastic workforce. How do you create enthusiasm?

How can you create enthusiasm?

Moving from a situation where you might be over-controlling your people is difficult, but straightforward. There are five steps to letting go and creating an enthusiastic workforce around you:

1) Take a timeout – sketch a way forward in just two hours
2) Reduce any anxiety about a change: assess team capability
3) Work on your own self confidence
4) Invest your personal energy in the project
5) Get them beyond 'I suck' – give them confidence

1) STOP! Take a timeout

You're overloaded with things to do, but you've got to just STOP for two hours. Switch off the BlackBerry and cellphone and log off from emails. Now, take a large sheet of paper (A3 works best, or flip chart paper) and, from memory, sketch out a timetable or mindmap – whatever works for you – of what your working week looks like. Do this from memory so that only the important things stick.

Now, redraft it – how do you **want** your week to look? Be as detailed and as creative as you'd like to be. You've got to back off from the day-to-day challenge, and think clearly what you want to do before you can move forward.

Hint 1: figure out when is your most productive time of day, when you're at your most alert and focused, and keep that for your prime business purpose. Don't waste your most productive time of day answering routine emails or phone calls.

Hint 2: Fill your calendar with higher level, strategic issues so that you won't be able to micromanage – because you won't have the time.

2) Reduce your anxiety over change – set a people strategy

If you are going to rely more on your people and your team in future, then you need to think in detail about your team. Before you can stop micromanaging and begin to pass on elements of your workload to them, you must assess whether your people are capable enough to move with you into a new way of working. Make notes on who among your people may need a coach or further training or who needs an external mentor. Discuss your ideas with them directly.

Consider which people you need to promote because there is nothing more they can learn with you. Consider also which people are performing below par and ask yourself how you'll increase their performance: by coaching from you? By development, off-the-job? Or, if necessary, by asking them to leave.

Work with your colleagues in Human Resources to refine and sharpen your people strategy and don't shy away from the difficult people decisions. Holding on to poor performers, for example, and working round them, sends a strong signal to other team members that you're not willing to take the tough decisions.

Finally get set to hire only great people. Simon Brown, VP of Brand Evangelism at Microsoft, says 'You've got to hire great people. Hire A people, A players. What I've found is that A players do themselves hire A players. They know what they're looking for. B players, on the other hand, only hire C players.' Only hire the best.

When you've got renewed confidence in your team, then is the time to begin the process of exciting them to higher levels of performance. Give away the elements of your job that you don't need to do. Give away the self-contained projects and parts of your job that add nothing to your senior role. Use the routine parts of your role to motivate your direct reports.

In turn you should urge them to give away elements of their roles to their direct reports. You shouldn't just dump on your direct reports. Define with them a zone where they can act independently. Expand the zone with every success and review it and consider shrinking it if they fail.

3) Work on your own self confidence

Expect that these changes will lead to discomfort during an adjustment period of anything from two to three months. But keep at it. Don't give up. If you keep at it you will all adjust. Get feedback from your team on how you're doing. Reward every positive step you take.

Train yourself to interpret the anxiety of not knowing every detail as a sign of progress towards becoming an inspirational leader.

Train yourself, also, to control your background thinking. Think and act as if outcomes were not life and death affairs. Care, but not too much. Get some perspective.

Remind yourself that everyone experiences failure and that failure is the best teacher.

Remind yourself that whatever your personal beliefs, research shows that perfectionists achieve less than people who approach their work in a relaxed fashion.

Test your appraisal of risk. If you delegate something and it isn't done well, will it really lead to a disastrous outcome? Is it possible that such a risk is worth it to develop other leaders?

Develop your sense of humor. Take your work seriously but don't take yourself too seriously. Laugh at work every once in a while. Your employees will enjoy seeing you as a human being with a sense of humour. This is perfectly professional.

Learn to take responsibility for what you *can* change and put the rest in the lap of fate. Concentrate on the important things and maybe the less important things will slot into place by themselves, like the final pieces of a jigsaw puzzle.

Seek professional help if necessary. You don't have to do this alone. Leading is one of the loneliest professions on the planet. Speak with a trained coach or psychologist to uncover the source of any anxieties that are holding you back.

Enlist the help of others in rolling out your new plans. Consider getting a coach or an external mentor to help you develop a plan to change your behaviour and to follow it through.

Who was it said the journey of a thousand miles begins with a single step?

4) Energise your people

Most people are motivated by the work they do, by having a rewarding and challenging job. It energises them. So how can you turn this to your advantage? How can you invest your personal energy in increasing the challenge of everyone around you?

Rob Cross is a professor at the University of Virginia's McIntire School of Commerce and Andrew Parker works with IBM's Knowledge and Organisational Performance Forum. Together they've developed an important idea they call buzz. 'Our high performers are not just people who are smart. We have some of the brightest consultants in the world here,' says Parker.

'But some are more successful than others, and it has much more to do with what I call buzz than a slight difference in IQ.'

Cross agrees: 'Our high performers create enthusiasm for things. I mean, they are smart and have good ideas, but more than that they are able to get people to buy into and take action on their ideas. They create energy, and even though this is intangible it generates client sales and follow-on work, as well as gets other people here engaged in and supportive of what they are doing. I know this might sound like a New Age idea, but what I call buzz or energy has a lot to do with these people's and ultimately IBM's success.'

So consider this: do you have buzz? Are you an energizer? When you walk into the office, does the energy level automatically rocket? Is there an unspoken and expectant buzz in the air: 'Something's going to happen!'

Inspirational Leadership
Blueprint Principle

Be an energiser

Or are you a de-energiser? A black hole? When you walk in the room does the energy level drain away through the floor? It's an interesting thought experiment to try. This is important in terms of enthusiasm because a common attribute of de-energizers is a single-minded focus on accomplishing tasks. Unfortunately, de-energisers not only drain the people they meet, but they can also affect the productivity of people they may not know.

Energisers, on the other hand, often accomplish more,

because they demonstrate attentiveness to the people around them. Energisers think of their work as a balance between tasks *and* relationships, and this is obvious in dozens of daily decisions and actions expressing a genuine concern for others.

Stopping to ask someone how he or she is doing (and being truly interested), recalling something important in that persons personal life, or shuffling tasks to accommodate someone in a moment of need are only a few of the small things that seem to come easily for energisers. Of course, these actions can't be scripted – they must be genuine. But they don't have to be lengthy. 'People often described to us five-minute hallway inter-actions that had a significant impact,' says Cross.

5) Get them past 'I suck' towards 'we rock'

One thing that builds enthusiasm without fail is having a cheer-leader for a boss. Not a relentless rah-rah-rah person. Just some-one who believes in the team. Someone who delegates to the team and believes in them. Someone who trusts them to per-form. This helps elevate a team beyond the level of 'I suck' through the layers of mediocre players into the category of play-ers who think highly of themselves. 'We rock' rather than I 'suck'.

At the time of the first Gulf War, when George Bush Senior occupied the White House, US citizens stopped flying to Britain. The classy hotels where Americans often stayed were suddenly empty as no one was flying east across the Atlantic. At the time Terry Holmes was General Manager of the Ritz Hotel on the edge of Piccadilly. Holmes is a tall man, broad chested, with a booming voice, and he was always impeccably dressed. In a crowded room you could always spy the grey, light check suit a head and a half above the other folks in the room. Holmes sensed that, with the numbers of guests at the hotel in freefall, morale was crashing. So he had small lapel pin badges made. He always carried some in his jacket pocket and if he hadn't seen a member of staff for a while he would go over to them, shake hands warmly and hand them a badge. The staff loved the badges and would wear them sometimes openly, sometimes pinned *behind* their lapels. And it became a secret symbol of unity for the porters, the night staff, housekeeping, catering and the rest of the staff, too. The badge said, in white block capital lettering on a red background. 'Tough times don't last forever. Tough people do.'

Holmes lived a positive approach and was always a positive supporter of the team. He wanted to take his people upwards to the next level and would always strive for excellence and wouldn't settle for 'competence'.

What can you do to help your team believe 'we rock'?

From micromanagement to enthusiasm

There's no trick to creating enthusiasm in the workplace. You just need a solid belief that the team can do what you ask them to do. All you can do is create a workplace where people can choose to invest their best efforts – or not. You can't dictate that they be enthusiastic. But you can stop killing their enthusiasm, by stopping the heavy levels of control that you may have used in the past. This will free up more time for you to focus on the things you should be focusing on, like getting round all your team and making sure they are energised by what you have to ask and say.

Do you remember the line 'How many psychiatrists does it take to change a lightbulb?' 'It doesn't matter,' goes the answer, 'but the lightbulb has to really want to change.' This reminds us that not everyone will be enthused or motivated by what you do or say. Don't beat yourself up over that. The whole point of letting people define their own goals and invest their own energy in their work is that it's their job to motivate themselves. All you have to do is create a climate where it's possible to do just that. So remember that people can only motivate themselves.

So in closing this chapter let's ask you – how do you motivate yourself at work? What motivates you? You have an important part to play as a role model. You ought to understand how you motivate yourself at work and why. Do you?

Turning to the three company failings

Enthusiasm brings to a close this section on the personal failings and the next three chapters address the much more challenging company failings. The first company failing is killing rewards.

THE FIFTH FAILING

Really Useless Leaders Kill Rewards

Really Useless Leaders use the wrong rewards, like money, for people who don't need it and they reward the wrong things, like safe investing, when they're trying to encourage risk taking

THERE ARE MYTHS ABOUT executive pay that are extremely dangerous. We know they are wrong and yet we still hold tight to them – we don't know what else to do. These myths form the backbone of a training programme called 'Compensation', headed by Stanford Business School's Jeffrey Pfeffer, a doyen among business school professors. Pfeffer has gravitas. He's knowledgeable. And he talks numbers, even when he's dealing with topics such as leadership and people strategy.

Describing his programme, Pfeffer is uncompromisingly blunt. 'Business people are adopting wrongheaded notions about how to pay people and why,' he says. 'In particular, they are subscribing to dangerous myths about pay.' The two myths relevant for us here are Pfeffer's critical top two: the myth that individual incentive pay improves performance (not everyone responds well to financial incentives) and the old chestnut, that people work primarily for the money. (Some do, but most in business do not.)

With increasing frequency, says Pfeffer, managers are harming their organisations by buying into and acting on these myths. Those that do, he warns, are doomed to endless tinkering with pay that will accomplish little, but cost a great deal. Part of the problem is that senior executives are blind when it comes to judging the motivation of others. They assume people in other parts of the firm are motivated the same way they are. But they aren't.

We won't go into Pfeffer's arguments here – this isn't a book about executive pay – but let's take it as read that there are motivators and rewards more valuable than money when it comes to inspiring the troops. With that said, let's look at the two most important tactics.

The power of recognition

At Deutsche Bank in the USA the Employee of the Month announcement is made, there are cheers, whoops and whistles. A great day for the employee – he or she was noticed! But at Deutsche Bank in Germany they resist the concept of 'Employee of the Month'. 'It just doesn't suit our culture,' Marianne told Steven on a leadership programme in Berlin recently.

'So why don't you have a different kind of recognition programme?' he asked. 'You could highlight teams rather than individuals, if personal visibility is the issue. And rather than posting a picture up in the lobby, why not capture the team's story on a blog, or in a practical written case study somewhere, so that others can learn from their technical expertise?' Marianne was writing notes as fast as she could. 'We'd never thought of these things, but yes I can see now these also are recognition, but in a different format.'

Recognising the value someone brings to the party is one of

the most powerful motivators that exists. Think back to a time someone praised you in an appropriate way, in an appropriate place. You may have felt so good you thought 'I could do this again!' which is precisely why we need to recognise people. They like it and it helps them focus on the tasks that managers want to see. People repeat the things that make them successful.

A word here for the managers who fear that offering too much recognition is a slippery slope. 'I recognise people in the pay packet at the end of the month,' one IT manager told us in Portugal. 'I don't need to keep saying "thank you", I expect people to provide a high level of service.' 'Saying "thank you" is just too "happy-clappy" for me,.' said another manager in a financial services organisation. All of which misses the point. Recognition is a different motivator from money. It fulfils a different need in those we recognise. And you don't have to pay the people you've recognised. Recognition – in that sense – is far better than money. It works for almost everyone albeit in different ways, it doesn't cost anything and the effects last far longer. (Is there a downside?)

Responsibility and power

What makes work worth doing? For more than 30 years, Professor John Hunt has been studying this question with a questionnaire – the Work Interest Schedule – that tens of thousands of people have completed around the world since it was first published in the 1970s.

Until Hunt launched the survey (fondly called 'the Wiz') there had been no easily accessible questionnaire able to provide information on what most (and least) motivated people in their choice of work or jobs or challenges. Now, however, with the data from managers in different sectors and different countries not only can we say with some certainty what drives people, we can also benchmark you against managers from those other sectors and countries. The survey is designed mainly for use in the classroom as a teaching tool and reveals the ten key factors that make us perform the way we do.

Factor 1: the search for financial gain to support our lifestyle
Factor 2: the desire for a quiet and calm, stress-free life
Factor 3: avoiding uncertainty or risk of poor infrastructure
Factor 4: clarity of goals and clear performance criteria
Factor 5: preference for working with others
Factor 6: a desire to be a team player
Factor 7: the desire for feedback and recognition from others
Factor 8: the drive for managerial power, dominance, control
Factor 9: the search for freedom and independence
Factor 10: the desire to stretch and challenge oneself

In programme after programme we've run using the WIS, managers are always surprised to learn that it isn't money that's the key driver for managers in business. Yes, it's power and responsibility – factor 8 – that excites most managers, men and women, whether they're based in the eastern hemisphere or the west. 'Their primary goal is managerial power,' says Hunt[14], 'the opportunity to influence, control and reward the behaviour of subordinates.'

**Inspirational Leadership
Blueprint Principle**

Most managers want power, responsibility or control

This isn't surprising when you consider that a company is a political institution where power is the life blood. Politics is only power in action and your ability to influence or coerce others adds to the formal authority you have. This increases your personal visibility and reach, and adds to the resources you can draw on or the size of your empire.

Before closing this chapter let's look briefly at the classic problems of reward from a strategic perspective. How can you make sure that you're rewarding the right thing?

The folly of rewarding A while hoping for B

'I got the best job in the world. An easy job disguised as a hard job.' Steve Kerr, an academic, a consultant and a practising manager, had just been appointed to run a little-known General Electric programme called Work-Out in southern California. Soon afterwards he worked very closely with Jack Welch, setting up GE's corporate university at Crotonville. He had attracted Welch's attention in part because of his main claim – a provocative paper called 'On the folly of rewarding A while hoping for B'. It's become a classic in motivation research and though it's 30 years old it still explains much of what's wrong with reward strategies in business today.

'Whether you're dealing with monkeys, rats or human beings,' says Kerr, 'it's hardly controversial to state that most organisms seek information concerning what activities are rewarded, and then seek to do (or at least pretend to do) those things.' Of course, how well this works depends on how much you want what's on offer, but basically this is the theory behind all incentive systems.

But there are plenty of examples of reward systems that are fouled up – the things that are rewarded are actually those which the person footing the bill actually wants to stop. What's worse is that often, on top of this, the behaviour that folks really want to encourage isn't being rewarded at all. isn't being rewarded at all. Take a look at this list.

We hope for...	But we often reward...
long-term growth; environmental responsibility	quarterly earnings
teamwork	individual effort
setting challenging 'stretch' objectives	making the numbers; achieving the goals
commitment to total quality	shipping on schedule, even with defects
candour; surfacing bad news early	reporting good news, whether it's true or not;
	and agreeing with boss, whether or not they're right

The reasons why we do these crazy things are straightforward, if a little stupid, says Kerr. Sometimes we pick the easiest thing to measure 'because we can'. Especially if it seems like an 'objective criterion'. We also overemphasise what we can see. For example, things like citizenship, teambuilding and creativity are hard to see so we don't measure or reward them. But just because something is hard to do doesn't mean we should take the easiest route out of the problem.

Overturning the wrong reward strategies

There are three steps to overturning poor reward strategies:

1) know your people, know their lifestyle and know the kinds of jobs they like. This is not just touchy feely stuff, but critical business knowledge. It will help you to prepare them for their next jobs. Get involved in succession planning, by the way. It's of major strategic importance..

2) recognise the value people bring to the party. People are less likely to leave a company if you're telling them how well they've done. So recognise the value they bring and be creative in how you do this. If the prevailing culture is not to celebrate the individual, recognize teams rather than individuals, or countries rather than teams.

3) assess which of your people are actively seeking more power and responsibility. This shouldn't be too hard, but do remember to chat to the introverts. They sometimes stay low profile but they need as much if not more recognition than the extroverts.

If Really Useless Leaders Kill Rewards and reward strategies, *useful* leaders need to be among the smartest and most creative in terms of motivating people. And the key is to know your people and know where they fit into the big picture. Much is known about reward and compensation, but managers need to become more sophisticated in their approach to reward. Treating reward as either carrot or stick is too basic for this day and age. Firstly, not all carrots are the same. People value different rewards. And secondly when you think of a carrot or a stick what does that remind you of? Perhaps there are better ways to think of employees.

THE SIXTH FAILING

Really Useless Leaders Kill Culture

*How can you build a high-commitment company culture
that delivers high performance?*

WHEN YOU BLOW A MILLION dollars on a CD-Rom
project that fails, you assume you're going to get fired.
That's what Terrell Jones thought when he worked at Sabre, the
computer-based reservation system originally developed by
American Airlines.

'I was sure I would be fired. Instead, my boss said "What did
you learn? Let's sit down and talk about how not to do it again."'

At American Airlines, says Jones, the company culture – the
routine way it worked – had an aspect of 'kill-the-messenger',
and so there were people who were afraid to take risks. It wasn't
like that in reality, he says, but that was the perception. 'American
Airlines was mainly a safety-first culture – and that's what you
want.'

But if you want innovation and risk taking, you have to allow
failure, says Jones, who went on to found online travel business

Travelocity and was president and CEO until 2002. 'Getting people to be okay with taking risk means celebrating the people who take risks,' says Jones. 'It means saying, "We tried it; it didn't work."'

You have to be willing to change things a few times to see if you can make them work, he suggests, but 'If you put out a flop, you can tell pretty quickly that it's just dead. So I tried to encourage people to fail fast and not agonise.'

But changing a culture that's risk averse to one that embraces risk is challenging to say the least. How should a new idea be protected from the defenders of the status quo? 'That takes upper management looking out for it,' says Jones. 'If senior managers want innovation, they've got to be able to put their finger on the innovation pulse. They have to be able to say "These are good ideas, and I want to protect them."'

Just as managers have accountability for the finances, Jones suggests that they should also have accountability for innovation. What are you doing to make innovation happen and to protect the early green shoots? You can't afford to have anyone say 'that'll never work round here', which unfortunately is all too common. What little things can you do to encourage new thinking? Or at the least trying new things to see if they work?

At Travelocity, there were weekly meetings where people would just talk about ideas. Middle managers would regularly be canvassing new ideas in brown bag lunches. 'When I did the meetings,' says Jones, 'I did them without any intervening managers in the room. I made sure managers here knew they had to be open to direct communication between line workers and the president of the company. If you don't make that clear, the intervening bureaucracy can kill the idea.'

Not only was Jones getting into the action of innovation

here, he was sending a very strong signal that he wouldn't be insulated from the people of the company. And this also reinforced the openness, reinforced the race to innovate and brought in new ideas.

Changing a company culture, the traditions that have developed over years or decades, is a real challenge. Most managers don't or can't change their cultures. We believe that Really Useless Leaders kill culture, they don't appreciate that the way we do things round here, the little routines and rituals that define the company, really matter. They act like a pair of handcuffs, chaining your company to the past.

You can see this best in the merger of two partners where real integration and the creation of a new, third business, different from the first two, never really happens. Instead the anecdotes and histories of the two distinctive companies remain in circulation simultaneously. Overcoming this cultural inertia is phenomenally difficult.

To make a start on reinventing the culture where you work take a look at some of the best company cultures out there and learn from them. Let's look briefly at what *Fortune* magazine regards as one of the best companies to work for in the world.

Building a 'work hard, play hard' culture

Biotechnology company Genentech, founded in 1976, ploughs up to 50% of its revenues back into research.[15] It's focused on what it calls 'significant unmet needs' in cancer research, immunology and tissue growth and repair. The projects (and the people) that don't fit this profile are removed and fiefdoms including product development and basic research are forced to work closely together. Like Google, Genentech encourages its scientists and engineers to spend fully 20% of each week pursuing pet projects. Then, once or twice a year, staff scientists and researchers must 'defend' their work before the Research Review Committee, a group of 13 PhDs that decides how to allocate the research budget. Some find the experience nerve-wracking, and that's ok, says the CEO Arthur Levinson. 'It should not be a cakewalk.'

Genentech's secret is its culture. And that is what propelled the company to the top of the list of Fortune's Best companies to work for in 2006. And while the culture attracts people to the company like moths to a light, getting into Genentech isn't easy. The company puts huge energy into hiring people – it's searching for people with passion and drive. For managers wanting to break in, it often takes five or six visits and maybe 20 interviews to win a job offer. The process screens out people hankering after salary, a fancy title and personal advancement. If candidates ask too many questions along those lines 'Boom! wrong profile,' says Levinson. But once they're in, there's another side to the company.

Every Friday night there's at least one beer festival or 'ho-ho' and every milestone calls for a party and a commemorative T-shirt. On very big occasions, there'll be a celebrity band – visitors have included Elton John and Mary J. Blige. And every few years Genentech awards sabbaticals to stave off burnout. After all, a 'work hard, play hard' culture can take its toll.

What's the message here? Well, Genentech gets it. Google gets it. Apple gets it. The obvious message is that culture is critical. It's critical to the way you compete. It's critical to the way you attract people into the business. And it's critical to the way you lead. But Genentech, Google and Apple also get perhaps the most significant point of all: that culture is not a single catch-all mission or vision statement bellowed down from the executive suite. Culture is founded on hundreds of tiny actions, from every manager and employee. And it's this that makes culture easy to influence but almost impossible to control. The answer is to just start things. Small things. That's all.

Psychologist Maja Storch, in *Scientific American*, describes our human needs as *short-term immediate* or *long-term habitual*.[16] 'Most individuals underestimate the power this factor can have in both their private and professional lives,' she says and this is a powerful message for those who want to influence company culture. 'One extravagant annual company picnic does not create a healthy working environment; it takes many immediate, smaller happy moments to achieve this atmosphere,' she says.

The *Fortune* magazine verdict on Genentech? 'Many corporations think it's terribly cutting-edge to maintain an arm's-length relationship with employees. Genentech wants you to move in.'

Don't kill culture, craft it

OK, so what can you do to influence the culture where you are? There is one simple thing that every individual can contribute that will influence company culture: new stories about the organisation. To change the company culture all you have to do is change the stories that people tell about the company. What do people say in the bar to a friend or family member about what it's like to work here. If you can change the stories, the culture of the place will inevitably change.

Here's the basic four-step process for influencing culture.

1) To change your company culture you've got to change the stories people tell about the organization, so you need to go on a Story Safari like we did in an earlier chapter.

2) To find your new stories, take a look at what the people in the

company are actually doing and it's likely that they'll be in the following three places:

a) find out what the company is starting? (And why?)

b) what is the company changing? (And why?)

b) what is the company stopping? (And why?)

3) Of the stories that you uncover, the stories that are symbolic will be most powerful. For instance, the Whitbread organization started life as a brewer of beers around 250 years ago. But in the last few years of the 20th century it stopped being a brewer to concentrate on a new portfolio of hotels, coffee bars and restaurants. However, the company was still headquartered at the very first brewery the company ever had in east London. The place was called The Brewery. However, it wasn't until CEO Alan Parker symbolically sold the Brewery and moved the HQ out of London that people finally started calling Whitbread a hospitality company (formerly a brewer), rather than a brewer (with hotel interests). There is still a long time to go before people no longer link Whitbread with brewing, but that's how long influencing culture can take.

4) Finally it is the routine actions that define a culture. The things that happen repeatedly. When Belmiro De Azevedo, the patriarch of Portuguese industrial conglomerate Sonae welcomes his staff to his palatial home he is welcoming the staff into his family. Regularly occurring social events like this can have an extraordinary quality. Starting or stopping certain actions will help define a new culture. But trying to institute systematic culture change programmes is fraught with difficulty. Companies that launch programmes under the banner of 'We are United' face immense difficulties, that's outside the scope of this book, though some of the resources at **www.7failings.com** will help. Visit 7failings.com and click on **FREE BOOK BONUSES**.

THE SEVENTH FAILING

Really Useless Leaders Kill Trust

What is the single most important thing that kills trust,
where and why does this affect the bottom line
and how can we build or rebuild trust, if at all?

GEOFFREY COLVIN FROM *FORTUNE* Magazine puts it this way: 'Trust is so fragile and so laboriously created that it may never extend very far in a top level team.'[17] This leads to the suggestion that maybe building a really high-performing executive team at the highest level is a mirage. It's not possible. 'It's just too hard to build more trust extensively at the top level where everyone is supposedly a star.'

Don't take Colvin's word for it. Study the extensive literature on team effectiveness, or discuss trust with sports teams, business teams or any other kind of team and it all comes down to this: trust is the backbone of the winning team. Which is why it's such a problem when Really Useless Leaders kill trust.

Dr Lawrence Levin, a construction industry consultant, points out that our personal experience of trust and – more often – distrust goes very deep. 'Trust involves risk and with it often a sense of great vulnerability – and we feel betrayal and tremendous anger when those bonds are broken.' With all of that going on in our minds, not to mention the impact of Enron and WorldCom on trust in corporations, you could be forgiven for thinking 'Why bother trusting anyone? Isn't it better to play your cards close to your chest?'

Well, not necessarily. Levin suggests that trust does have a significant commercial return on investment and you can also point to the significant costs of trust when you *don't* have it. For instance, a reputation for making huge layoffs creates a poor reputation as an employer. It means it takes longer to hire great people. 'The cost of replacing someone is at least one year's salary,' says Levin, 'plus the expensive indirect costs such as the learning curve for new staff, organisational memory, morale, internal and customer relationships and so on. The character of a company and of its management is a selling point to potential recruits. A bad track record is often difficult to recover from.'

More importantly, the impact of losing trust on commitment and loyalty is huge. 'We ask people to work monster hours, to be committed to their work, to subscribe to the values of the firm,' says Levin. 'Ask yourself why an employee should be more committed to your firm than your firm is to her?' In other words, there are huge overt and hidden costs of an employee who is only just doing what is expected of him or her. Extensive studies show that retaliation in the form of absenteeism and theft are common in companies where trust is low or non-existent.[18]

'Generally,' says Levin, 'the result of low trust is classic passive or aggressive behaviour and work slowdown.'

What is trust? And where is it?

Before we explore in more detail the biggest single killer of trust, let's just make sure we agree what trust is, because when you start thinking about it, many different explanations come to mind.

One important aspect of trust, for instance, is reliability. Can I rely on someone to deliver what they say they will? When they don't deliver, my trust in them ebbs away and I feel betrayed. The payoff is that I'm reluctant to give work to them again, especially if it's innovative or critical work for our company. Also, I'm reluctant to promote someone I can't rely on because I can't guarantee the quality of their service to my colleagues, my bosses or our customers.

Another challenge for managers today is highlighted by this story from Katrina, a manager in pharmaceutical sales in Switzerland. 'If I know where my kids are, if I know who they're with and if I know they've got a mobile phone switched on then I'm at ease. I don't need to be with them every minute. It's the same with my boss. If I can see – or think I can, or would be able to if I wanted to – all of what my boss was up to, I'd trust him. Nothing to think over, nothing to manage.'

So another issue is if you've got transparency, there's trust. No transparency, no trust. End of issue. Sometimes we forget there is no such thing as 'half transparency'. If there's just one element of transparency missing, then there's no transparency, no trust.

The next step is to think for a moment where is trust, actually? And the straightforward answer is that it's in the relationship. Trust is in the relationship between two people, or teams, or companies, or countries. And so the elements we've been discussing here, such as reliability and transparency, apply to the relationship. If you lose trust in someone the relationship breaks down. Some experts even regard trust AS the relationship. This doesn't quite work, however, as you can have a difficult relationship with someone or with some company. But it is true to say that you can't have a meaningful relationship with someone you don't trust. Which leads naturally to the next question: how do our relationships of trust break down?

The fastest killer of trust

The most significant killer of trust in all the conversations we've had with people over three years is none of the things we've discussed so far. The trust killer above all others is – unusually perhaps – being unfair. Some academics call it 'justice' or 'equity' (though not in a financial sense). But fairness is what they're talking about. And within the broad topic of fairness, the main thing that kills people's trust is perceived unfairness over pay.

This is sometimes misinterpreted by managers as people squabbling over more money, but as we discussed earlier people aren't necessarily motivated by money. No, the question is one of fairness and equality. Equal pay for women and men doing the same role is an important issue. Equal pay for people who've been doing a role for some time and those joining from outside at 'market rates' (though they might be younger or less experienced) is an important issue. But these are not questions about the quantity of money. They are questions about fairness.

An exchange Steven was involved in highlights the significant fall-out for companies when people think you're being unfair. 'I was livid!' hissed Martine, a training manager in the IT industry. The voices were hushed round the coffee machine as she spoke. 'I've just found out that Mike, who I've been training for the last seven months, has asked for an extra £14,000 or he'll leave.' Her colleague Christopher asked 'What happened?' 'Well,' said Martine, 'they paid, didn't they. I couldn't believe it. I'll stay, but the first chance I get, I'm off. I've still got to train him even though he gets paid much more than I do.' Within six months Martine had left the company.

Coincidentally, Martine's colleague Christopher, head of the department, had another manager parachuted in above him and so was demoted to deputy manager shortly after this conversation. He also left the team, leaving the department short-staffed and in limbo.

Inspirational Leadership
Blueprint Principle

The fastest single killer of trust
is not being fair

So be scrupulously fair
in everything you do – from hiring to firing

While this company suffered the catastrophe of losing two people, other organisations can make mistakes with fairness that affect many more people, sometimes the whole organisation.

'It is absolute insanity to pay out seven-figure bonuses at a time when the company is suffering nine-figure losses, is mired in eleven-figure debt and is seeking further help from it's employees to survive for the long term,' said Ralph Hunter, president of the Allied Pilots Association[19]. He had discovered that about 1,000 American Airlines bosses were to get huge stock-based bonuses when the company had lost more than $7 billion in the previous five years. Four bosses would get more than $1 million each.

No one is disputing the need to attract, keep and reward senior executives, but 'This is very poor timing of the management bonuses and isn't in the best interests of the company and the employees,' said Tommie Hutto-Blake, president of the Association of Flight Attendants.[20]

In short, leaders and the HR teams who manage payroll and salary adjustments must understand how much unfair decisions on pay, or even decisions that are *perceived* as unfair, kill trust.

The challenge of managing fairness

Creating trust in your organisation is not easy, and like culture it's extremely difficult to manage, no matter how carefully you prepare for it. One international company we know decided the way it rewarded staff was unfair, so it set about trying to rebuild trust with a brand new system that was transparent, fair and reliable. The system was guaranteed to increase trust in the organisation, thought the senior executive team, and it would automatically increase morale and performance all round. The aspiration was high, but in the end the reality didn't match these expectations.

In the past, the company had given a salary increase to all staff, and then topped that up with 'secret bonuses' for a few people hand-picked by individual managers. This merit system was obviously open to abuse: it let managers reward their favourites, and 'punish' those people they didn't like.

So the company decided all staff would now be given one of five grades, ranging from excellent at the top to unsatisfactory at the bottom. The people judged to be 'excellent' would get a bonus of, say, 5% on top of their salary increase. The 'satisfactory' people would get 3% and the 'unsatisfactory' people wouldn't get anything except for the general salary increase, which in their case would be reduced by a percentage point, depending on inflation at the time.

This is a fairer system, the company thought. 'We'll be rewarding the best people, everyone will know why, and everyone will be motivated and happy.' The first step was telling the line managers they had to grade all their staff. 'You have to find a certain percentage of your people "excellent" and a certain proportion "unsatisfactory".' The line managers shifted a little in their seats. Then Ulrich spoke up and the floodgates opened.

'But all my staff are excellent,' said Ulrich. He was a senior division head with many years' experience and highly regarded by the board. 'If any of them were unsatisfactory, I'd have sorted it out years ago.' The Executive Board said he *had* to find some unsatisfactory people in his department. But Ulrich – and others – refused to budge. Despite this setback, the company pressed ahead with a series of short staff briefings. Which turned into marathons.

At the open staff meetings, a line of bosses sat in a row at the front of the room to explain the new system to the staff. Before the meeting they expected resistance from the people likely to be given the lowest grade, and from the moment the meeting started they were under attack. But not from the 'unsatisfactory' workers. They were attacked by their star performers, the employees who would most likely be graded 'excellent'!

The high performers were really unsettled, on their own behalf as well as for others in the business. 'How are we going to be graded?' they asked. 'Who's going to make the decisions?' 'How can they be fair?' Somebody at the back chipped in 'How come every single team has to have some "unsatisfactory" people?' 'How can we appeal against the decision?,' asked another. 'What's the difference between an excellent worker with a 5% bonus, and a good worker with a 3% bonus?' Everyone agreed the system was simply not fair. Or rather that while it may have been fairer in principle, employees felt there was too much sub-jectivity in the whole thing and that it was open to more abuse than the old 'secret bonus' system.

The system was allowed to limp along for a year, but because of the concerns about fairness and the fact that trust in manage-ment was at an all-time low, the insistence on quotas for each grade was dropped. It was no surprise when, the year afterwards, the whole thing was completely dropped, having demoralised the star performers, the line managers, the leadership team and — well, everyone.

There are many lessons from this company's experience. But above all it teaches the significance of fairness and *perceived* fair-ness as it relates to the issues of pay and performance ratings. This seems to generate the greatest heat in conversations about trust. But don't forget the apparently trivial issues of who gets gadgets (the BlackBerry wars), or who gets the nearest car park-ing slots to the entrance, or who gets the corner office also mat-ter to a surprising degree. Why is this?

These things matter because we are so conscious today of success and achievement that the pay and perks that companies give us become really significant, but not in themselves. They matter because they actually represent 'us' and symbolise our public status, so we're highly conscious of them. In part it's about saving face.

Building trust in your leadership style

You're a smart manager so by now you've got the message. You won't make the mistake of thinking that trust is a touchy feely, warm and fluffy, optional extra. You know it's the backbone of your leadership style and that you need to make every effort to build trust in you. But you'll also recognise how difficult it is to manipulate, or even to influence trust in a relationship. So don't try to strait-jacket trust with systems. Instead, review the following tactics and strategies and build trust through your own simple actions. Because trust has to be built and earned, not imposed and administered.

How to build trust

If as we said earlier, trust is in our relationships – the connections between two people, teams or companies – then building trust is as simple as changing the quality of our relationships. Sounds simple doesn't it? But we know it isn't that easy.

What all the tactics and strategies below involve is investing effort and energy in strengthening our relationships. It's about giving time and sometimes resources to the people we value. Sometimes it's about taking things out of a relationship, doing less for people, and we've touched on that throughout this book, especially in Chapter 4 on micromanagement and enthusiasm.

Sometimes building trust is about forgiveness, reaching out to forge new connections where relationships have failed in the past. Anyone following the strained negotiations between peoples in the Middle East, or Africa, or Indonesia, knows this is not easy. But does that mean we shouldn't try? Of course not. But it will take determination and skill.

1) THINK: Get the executive team together to discuss trust

You've got to discuss jointly the issue of trust and what you're going to do about, if anything, with the people who best represent your organisation. Explore the issue of fairness and how you're going to be scrupulously fair in everything you do. You need a real dialogue about how you bring this set of values to life. So get an outside perspective by asking customers, employees and other external stakeholders what they think. Ask them to be honest. Then decide on clear operating procedures and above all open channels of communication with your people. This is about **engagement** with the senior executive team.

2) TALK: Get the executive team walking the talk

Your people and external stakeholders need to know what's going on. So get your executive out in front and communicate – we're talking true dialogue here, so listening is the order of the day. An honest exploration of the **emotions** associated with business is important, but the key is **explanation**. Let people know what's going on. Remember that people will be watching what you do next, especially when trust is low. Credibility is key here – 'say' must equal 'do'. Commitments build trust.

3) ACT: The fastest way to get trust is to give trust.

We know that the fastest way to get trust is to give trust. So involve your people in delivering the performance required. Don't micromanage them, but find out what they can do for the business and give them the resources to make it happen. People have such **enthusiasm** for their roles you only need to guide that to create a high performance, high commitment organisation champing at the bit.

Is trust a problem for companies? You bet. According to a survey by the UK's Chartered Institute of Personnel and Development, only one in four employees trust senior management to look after their interests. Research company MORI is more damning. Nine out of ten people believe that company directors cannot 'be trusted to tell the truth'. Some managers may be questioning whether this really matters? After all, in spite of the low esteem that politicians and company executives are held in, the world's democracies and capitalism generally seem to be ticking along pretty well, apart from a few 'challenges' in the Middle East, Indonesia and Africa.

Yes, it matters, says Richard Reeves, Director of Intelligence Agency, an ideas consultancy.[21] 'Lack of trust does matter because firms that are not trusted will have to be regulated more rigorously, which pushes up their costs as well as adding to the burden on taxpayers.' This is profit-making or profit-breaking stuff, says Reeves. 'Companies with trusting cultures are more efficient, both because information flows more freely and because less management time and effort is devoted to surveillance and conflict resolution.' (So even if cynical senior executives don't buy the 'trust is good' mantra for its own sake, they should buy it because it will save them time and money.)

Keep talking

It's fitting that we close this chapter, the most important in the book, talking about trust. Because trust is about talking. Talking not so much about 'Do we or don't we?', or 'Should we or shouldn't we?' Talking about trust is a matter of 'How will we?'

Whatever you call it, talk, conversation or dialogue is the key to overcoming all of the Seven Failings. It's also much more than that. Because talk is what we fundamentally do. For us, talk is action. It's what makes us uniquely human. Talk was the first tool we ever had and it's still the most important human tool. We should use it to build and strengthen our human relationships – with our friends and family and colleagues, and with those who are not friends, with those we don't trust, where there is a history of betrayal.

We're not saying that trusting someone when there is a history of treachery and deceit between you is easy. Far from it. We're not saying that Palestinians and Israelis, Bosnian Serbs and Muslims, bankers and their bankrupt clients, and spouses rushing toward divorce can simply brush away their past, their fears, and their suspicions.

But talking about trust, and believing that trust is possible, even in the face of extreme and vehement distrust, is the first and essential step. And while the talk between you may begin with venom and with mutual accusations these can, when mediated well, lead to negotiations. Skilful negotiations can then lead to mutual commitments. Small at first, but they do build trust. And while mutual commitments and their fulfilment may never completely put an end to distrust, they do build trust, a real and authentic trust. And authentic trust has its eyes wide open.

Authentic trust is a delicate combination of trust and distrust. It's better than blind faith, which is naive and foolish because it pretends distrust doesn't exist.

So to talk about trust is to recognise, first and foremost, that whether we like it or not, we are in this together. Whether 'this' is a marriage, a business relationship, a corporation, a community, a continent, or the world. And trusting relationships, no matter how tentative, are always better than war.

Personal review questions

1) What does trust mean to you? Where, when and why does it matter?

2) Who do you respect and trust? Why? What is it about specific people that helps you trust them? (Be specific.)

3) How much does your team lose when trust is weak or missing? In what areas would greater trust improve performance, for example strengthening customer loyalty or increasing innovation?

THE EIGHTH FAILING

Really Useless Leaders Kill Action

Don't procrastinate, do it now.
Or 'How much change are you prepared to embrace?'

WHAT WE'VE SHOWN WITH this book is that the Seven Failings of Really Useless Leaders are significant barriers to performance. Remove the barriers and productivity and profitability will inevitably increase.

We've also shown that overcoming the Seven Failings is difficult, but it's not impossible and the key is trust. What's more, while creating innovative reward strategies, influencing company culture and influencing trust are things that need to happen at a company-wide level, you personally can make a difference by addressing the personal failings that are totally within your control. In fact, we're coming to the conclusion that it's only by addressing the four personal failings – explanation, emotion, engagement and enthusiasm – that we can create a high performing, high commitment organisation in the first place. In other words, sort out your personal failings and the company failings will sort themselves out.

Some managers will still be cynical and it's easy to be cynical. Many have tried to define a leadership strategy that inspires their people. What we've done, though, is draft a simpler guideline for what leadership can be. Do less and get more out of your people. But this takes courage.

Have you got the strength to lead?

What's the alternative? Well, you don't have to take our advice. You can continue to offer partial and incomplete explanations that confuse people and don't align their efforts on the company's goals.

You can continue to show a lack of empathy for where employees are in their lives and work, lowering their willingness to work harder for you.

You can continue to set objectives and targets that don't engage your people because they're not stiff enough.

And you can micromanage them to within an inch of their lives, so they see no value in innovating or taking productivity to the next level.

You can believe that people are only interested in money, and so demotivate them by not giving them incentives more valuable than money.

You can anchor company culture in the past, without realising that what got you 'here' won't get you 'there'.

And you can forget that the most important aspect of any relationship between people is trust.

Who needs trust when you can tell people what to do, right? Leadership is about dictating what to do and focusing on execution, execution, execution, yes?

Or you can answer the following questions:

1) EXPLANATION: How and when do you set the vision for your projects? How much do you allow input?

2) EMOTION: How does emotion shape your management style? How do you deal with people who are different from you?

3) ENGAGEMENT: How much do you engage your team in goal setting? How much do you allow the team to measure its own performance? How and when do you review performance? How much do you learn from mistakes as well as success?

4) ENTHUSIASM: How do you motivate yourself at work? How do you create the freedom or climate where people can motivate themselves?

5) REWARDS: How creative are you in the reward strategies you use? How many rewards, other than money, do you use? How do you know you're using the right reward for the right person at the right time?

6) CULTURE: How much do you personally influence culture? What can you do to create new stories?

7) TRUST: How can you win the trust of your people? If the fastest way to get trust is to give trust, what could you give away or stop doing that would increase trust in you?

Answer these questions, put your answers into action and yours will most likely become a great company to work for.

You see these inspirational surveys every year don't you – such as the 'World's Most Admired Company', 'The 100 Best

Companies to Work For'. And you may have wondered, unless you're already in there, if it's worth the effort of doing all the fancy things you need to do to get in there? In other words, does being a 'great company to work for' actually affect performance and productivity? There's a very clear answer.

Ingrid Fulmer of Michigan State University, Barry Gerhart of the University of Wisconsin-Madison and Kimberly Scott of the William Wrigley Jr Company wondered whether the *Fortune* survey 'The 100 Best Companies to work for in America' might be useful for more than just selling advertising[22]. 'For instance, might the list represent a tool that investors could use to gauge the value and condition of what many executives claim is their most important asset: people? And are the additional costs associated with being a great place to work (eg outstanding pay and benefits) justified by higher firm performance?'

Their detailed financial analyses showed that over the six years they studied (1995-2000), the 100 best companies had:

- a higher return on assets than their peer comparison firms
- higher market-to-book ratios
- cumulative stock returns that outperformed peer firms
- cumulative stock returns that outperformed a composite index
- higher annual returns in five years out of six
  (significantly higher in two years)
- better market returns in four out of six years
  (significantly better in one year)

They concluded that 'Best companies to work for' can expect lower turnover of people, increased commitment and better work performance. They will also be able to attract better employees from the market, be more innovative generally, more creative and have a fantastic pool of talented executives to draw on for succession planning.

So yes, while it costs more in the immediate short term to be a great company to work for, there is a rapid payoff in market and financial terms as well as in managing your people's enthusiasm and engagement with the business.

Your Inspirational Leadership Blueprint

You must believe that your leadership matters. You've got to set your Inspirational Leadership Blueprint for success. You can make a difference if you stop doing the seven things that hinder performance and productivity And for this book to have been any value at all, you have to do something now. You have to act. Maybe there are elements of your leadership style you want to drop. Maybe there are some things you want to tweak. But whatever you do, do something.

We said earlier that Stephen Covey now has an Eighth Habit of Really Effective People, so we feel completely justified in having an Eighth Failing. And the Eighth Failing of Really Useless Leaders is this: not doing anything about the other seven. In other words, Really Useless Leaders kill action. They procrastinate, they sit on their hands. After reading this book, however, you won't do that will you?

So what are going to do now?

Visit **7failings.com** *and click on*
FREE BOOK BONUSES
for free resources as well as
more information on what to do now

APPENDIX ONE

How We Studied The Seven Failings

L ET'S GET THIS STRAIGHT at the outset: we didn't start out with the intention of assessing what leaders do well or badly. We didn't set out to define the tactics and strategies of inspirational leadership. And we certainly haven't been categorising our coaching clients or the managers on our executive education programmes. ('She's a good leader, he's a useless leader..., useless leader..., good leader...') No, this book simply emerged from the work we've been doing and the questions we've been asking over the past six years. But the book – light-hearted though it is – is grounded in solid research, research that is being reported, in a much drier style, in the academic literature.

Our primary research was conducted in two distinct phases, firstly from 2000 to 2003 and then from 2003 to 2007. In the first phase we were engaged with a lengthy and in-depth study of a single professional service firm. This firm had around 1000 employees and operated mainly in Europe and the Far East. We were granted access to all the senior managers over an extended period of time and were able to shadow the most senior among them for many hours if not days at a time. We had intimate access to the thoughts and thought processes of the senior management team, conducting semi-structured interviews repeatedly with the 12 most senior directors in the service firm. In total there are hundreds of hours of narrative interview data.

In addition, we were given privileged access to shareholder meetings and quarterly business review meetings, which were also recorded, and to the assessment of the most senior 40 managers in the business through psychometric instruments. We also were able to shadow and audio or videotape the actions of various members of the senior management team over a two-year period.

At the end of this first phase we constructed the first frameworks for what eventually became our Inspirational Leadership Blueprint. This work partly inspired our last book, *Leadership Unplugged*, which explored the language of leadership and how senior executives use strategic conversation to influence and inspire their people.

But all of this work was, so far, based on data from a single company. To see if it might apply in other companies – to test for generalizability – we began two separate explorations between 2003 and 2007. We undertook a literature review of all the motivation research that existed – a review that encompassed many hundreds of studies between 1987 and 2007 – and we framed what we believed to be the seven building blocks of strategic conversation. There is rich supporting evidence in dozens of studies – some of which are quoted in this book – for the Inspirational Leadership Blueprint we've developed.

To test the Blueprint further, we looked to data we collected from questionnaires and from informal, unstructured interview data from organisations we worked with in the UK, Germany and Portugal. We hoped to be able to show that managers were indeed using the language techniques we had identified to inspire and motivate their people. The thousand managers we talked with and interviewed over the past four years told us honestly about their strong feelings and unique experiences of good and poor leaders.

What this second phase showed, however, was something else. These data showed that, despite most managers today being much more highly educated than managers in the past, there were still major shortcomings in the leaders in our businesses. In other words, while managers may know *what* to do to lead their people – enthuse their staff, be more emotionally intelligent and so on – the actual experience of managers on our programmes was that the managers back at the ranch still didn't know *how* to lead as well as they could. That is, they didn't know, couldn't do it or wouldn't do it. And there were many reasons for these failings.

So we decided to report these findings not as yet another sugar-coated positive psychology text, exhorting managers to inspire their people by drawing on Martin Luther King and Mahatma Gandhi as role models. Rather – somewhat tongue-in-cheek – we've written the story as a reminder that many of us still struggle to lead, preferring the tyranny of 'JFDI' because we think it's more effective.

It also explains why there is much less focus in this book on the whys and the whats of leadership and much more on the hows. How can leaders create the belief that managers truly have personal control, support and freedom? It also explains why there are few quotes and stories here from the WASP-ish CEOs that grace the covers of *Fortune,* The *Financial Times* and *Business Week.* They were never the core of this research study.

Instead we've concentrated on the unsung middle and senior managers who we work with on a daily basis, whose insights and experience make up the bulk of this book. Without them this book would not have been written and this book is written for them.

In conclusion, while our findings are largely inductive and have emerged from our observations of managers and discussions with managers in many different companies, we have also drawn on and benefited from the work of many other scholars. We acknowledge this debt to our secondary research sources in our references and endnotes. If the work you hold in your hand has any value it is because their insights have been invaluable to us in interpreting and understanding our data. We hope that this book will strengthen the call for greater academic and managerial attention to inspirational leadership as the vital source of individual performance, and therefore of corporate productivity and profitability.

APPENDIX TWO

Special Bonus Offer
Steven Sonsino's Inspirational Leadership Blueprint Workshop — Free

A S A THANK YOU for buying *The Seven Failings of Really Useless Leaders*, Jacqueline Moore and Steven Sonsino are offering a scholarship for you and a colleague or friend to attend the two-day Inspirational Leadership Blueprint Workshop as Steven Sonsino's guests. That is a total value of at least £3994 – for free.

These guest seats are available only to purchasers of *The Seven Failings of Really Useless Leaders*, published by MSL Publishing and printed by Cambridge University Press. The course must be completed by January 1 2008, and this offer is made on a space-available basis. In addition, you should know that all seating is first-come, first-served. To assure your spot, please register immediately at **www.7failings.com**.

At the Inspirational Leadership Blueprint Workshop you will expand on the insights provided in this book by transforming your leadership style and taking your leadership career to the next level. You will learn:

1) How to inspire greater performance from your people – how to use the right strategies for inspiring all employees to higher levels of productivity and profitability.

2) How to make more money for yourself and your business by boosting your own inspirational leadership style – in other words, how to convert your current role into one that makes even more money for you, your teams and your company.

3) How to influence the senior executives in your life – how to get your own boss, as well as other senior stakeholders, to listen to and act on your advice by identifying and understanding their key needs and 'hot buttons'.

4) How to find and use the nine motivators more valuable than money to create high-performance and high-commitment from your team.

5) How to use the secret power of money and motivate your people as never before – it doesn't matter how much or how little you have in the budget, money can motivate your people, but only if you use it well.

6) And you will find out how to build a compelling leadership brand that takes your career to the next level – winning in your current job depends on your motivational leadership skills, but winning your next role depends on your leadership reputation.

Over this intensive two-day programme you will learn how to develop your personal Inspirational Leadership Blueprint which will help you to increase your time, money and freedom. You will learn how to integrate all aspects of inspirational leadership in a consistent and systematic way and take your career to the next level

In short, you will learn how to inspire your people to higher levels of performance, productivity and profitability.

If you are currently a senior executive, a middle-manager or a serial entrepreneur, and if you're not 100% satisfied with your career track to date, and if you know you have more potential than your results are showing, then register for the Inspirational Leadership Blueprint Workshop today. This programme will change your leadership success and your career path. Register now at **www.7failings.com**.

Inspirational Leadership
Blueprint Certificate

Steven Sonsino and Moore Sonsino Limited invite you and one colleague or friend to attend the Inspirational Leadership Blueprint Workshop as our guests. To register, and for more information, go to **www.7failings.com**.

If you have no access to a computer call us on +44(0)1234 771100 and we'll gladly register you.

Notes

This offer is open to all purchasers of *The Seven Failings of Really Useless Leaders* by Jacqueline Moore and Steven Sonsino. Original proof of purchase is required. The offer is limited to the two-day Inspirational Leadership Blueprint Workshop only and your registration in the seminar is subject to availability of space and/or changes to the programme schedule.

The workshop must be completed by January 1 2008. Corporate or organizational purchasers may not use one book to invite more than two people.

While participants will be responsible for their own travel and other costs, admission to the programme is complimentary. Participants in the workshops are under no additional financial obligations whatsoever to Steven Sonsino or Moore Sonsino Limited.

Moore Sonsino Limited reserves the right to refuse admission to anyone it believes may disrupt the workshop and to remove from the premises anyone it believes is disrupting the workshop.

APPENDIX THREE

Share Your
Leadership Lessons

THIS BOOK TEACHES YOU to observe and reflect on your ways of thinking about leadership. We want to challenge your limiting thoughts, habits and actions with regard to the leading of other people. We want you to put people first. Really to put people first and to mean it. Leadership is often one of the biggest areas of pain in people's working life. But, as always, there's a bigger picture to consider. You see, once you start recognizing your non-supportive ways around leadership, this awareness transfers into every other part of your life.

The goal of this book has been to raise your consciousness to your own strengths and perhaps to some of your weaknesses. And that awareness means observing and reflecting on your own thoughts and actions. We want you now to make conscious authentic choices about your leadership style. You can choose how to act. We don't want you to be trapped by the neural programming of your past life. So this book is a challenge to you to live your life as a higher, more authentic self, rather than to act from your fear-based, previous self. Be the best you can be and take charge of your career and life. But you know what? The heart of this transformation is not just about you. It is about the people in your team, your business and your life. Our world is nothing more than the collection of people and relationships we interact with. And as each individual raises his or her consciousness – moving from fear to courage, from control to collaboration – then our personal network raises its consciousness.

If you want your personal world to operate in a certain way, then your logical starting point is for you to operate that way. If you want your team, or your business, or even your family to operate in a certain way, then again the logical starting point is for you to become an even better manager or leader. We believe it's your duty to develop yourself to your fullest potential, to create success in your life however you define success. And in so doing, you will be able to help others and add to your personal world in a substantial and positive way.

We therefore ask you to share this message of courage with others. Get the message of this book out to as many people as you can. Commit to telling at least one hundred of your colleagues and associates, friends and family about it or consider getting it for them as a life-changing gift. Not only will they be introduced to powerful leadership concepts, they will learn to observe the way they think, raise their consciousness, and in turn raise the consciousness of your personal network. It would also be incredible for them to join you at the Inspirational Leadership Blueprint Workshop. It is truly powerful to have your colleagues or friends share such an extraordinary experience with you. Our dream is that one book, one course, one person at a time we can make a difference. We can change the world for the better. We ask for your support in making this dream a reality. Thank you.

Jacqueline Moore and Steven Sonsino

APPENDIX FOUR

Recommended Resources

The Inspirational Leadership Blueprint Workshop
Two days

The Inspirational Leadership Blueprint Workshop will transform your leadership style and take your leadership to the next level. On this intensive two-day workshop you will learn how to inspire your people to higher levels of performance, productivity and profitability. Whatever stage you're at in your career, the Inspirational Leadership Blueprint Workshop will work for you.

If you want to take your leadership success to the next level then check the city-by-city schedule at the main website: **www.7failings.com**.

Inspirational Leadership Blueprint
Evening Classes and Teleseminars

The principles of the Inspirational Leadership Blueprint are taught in evening lectures across the world and also in teleclasses or teleseminars.

For details and schedule go to the web: **www.7failings.com**.

Leadership Theatre — how to boost your performance when you're onstage all the time
Three days

Have you ever thought that as a leader you're on-stage all the time? There is no off-stage when you're a leader. If you want to develop your day-to-day physical presence and have greater impact, without pretending to be someone you're not, and if you want to be a memorable and remarkable leader, then Leadership Theatre will help you. This programme is NOT about presenting, but it will help you to become a better presenter.

Leadership Theatre is an intensive three-day workshop where we explore all the brief encounters you have with your people and help you significantly improve how you personally communicate and how you come across – in one-to-one conversations, in group presentations and meetings, and in your major platform speeches. If you're a leader who is onstage all the time, join us for Leadership Theatre – the science and art of boosting your personal performance.

For details and a schedule: **www.7failings.com**.

The Leadership Mentoring Programme
Teleclasses and teleseminars

If you want to develop your leadership impact in your business, and you want more personal attention, you will find the more intimate Leadership Mentoring Programme a practical alternative. This will also be the programme of choice for leaders who can't make any of the dates for the Inspirational Leadership Blueprint.

Over a five week programme of web-based and telephone classes Steven Sonsino helps you to review and improve your leadership impact.

For details and a schedule go to the main website at **www.7failings.com**.

Choose – The Life Directions Workshop
Two days

If you feel uncertain about your future direction – in your work or personal life – then join us on 'Choose', the Life Directions' workshop. Over two intensive days you will develop new insights into your present life, and will develop new meaning and purpose to enable you to make clearer choices about what to do in the future. If you want to create a tangible framework for your future life, or if you just want greater focus and clarity in your life, and if you want to know how to do it successfully, then choose 'Choose', the Life Directions workshop.

For details and a schedule go to **www.7failings.com**.

The FastTrack Business School

Five days

You don't have an MBA and you don't have the time to give up a year or two to do a part-time executive programme. But you worry that you're missing out on the latest strategy and marketing tools, finance for non-financial managers and on the latest leadership skills.

If this sounds like you then join us at the FastTrack Business School, a five-day guerrilla bootcamp, where our world-class faculty will give you the latest practical tools and tactics from the business school world. We guarantee you'll get no useless theory, but there will be all the essential theory you need, as well as all the practical tactics and strategies to help you to make a tangible difference in the workplace and to your career.

For details and a schedule: **www.7failings.com**

Train the Trainer

Four days

Earn additional income while you teach what you love. That's exactly what you'll learn at our Train the Trainer Workshops. Learn everything you need to be successful in the training business, including choosing the right topic, designing an incredible programme, using accelerated-learning techniques and marketing for success. By the end of this programme you will be an enthusiastic trainer who knows exactly how to transform the careers and lives of your clients.

For details and a schedule: **www.7failings.com**

Leadership Coaching and Mentoring
Ongoing

The best athletes, actors and executives in the world all have one thing in common – they have great mentors. Have you got the courage to work closely in an ongoing coaching or mentoring relationship with Steven Sonsino? This programme is not for the faint-hearted. Steven is a demanding and provocative mentor and he doesn't accept everyone as a client.

Visit **www.7failings.com** for more details and to find out how to apply.

The Leadership Success Retreat
Five days

Over the years, we've conducted hundreds of training pro-grammes, but nothing compares to the week-long, life-changing experience we have in store for you in 2008. We've combined all of our developmental exercises, personal learning modules, and small group activities into an astounding five-day programme.

On Day One, we'll determine what you want from life. Then, over the next four days, we'll work together to help you bring out the authentic person you really are, someone who can confident-ly create and pursue their goals.

We guarantee you've never attended anything that will have this much impact on your life and career.

For details and a schedule: **www.7failings.com**

Home Learning Programmes

Many of the programmes described here are available on CDs or DVDs, many include CD-Roms, so you can learn at your own pace, in your own home, or office, or even in the car.

For full details go to **www.7failings.com**.

Leadership.FM
The Most Popular Leadership Podcast on iTunes

To hear or see Steven Sonsino's leadership podcasts at your PC or ready to download to your iPod, visit **www.leadership.fm**. In six short months, Leadership FM became the most popular leadership podcast on the Apple iTunes Store. Find out why by going to **www.leadership.fm**, or subscribe via Apple iTunes. It's free.

Speaking Engagements

The single word that people tend to use when they hear Steven Sonsino speak is 'inspirational'. His leadership message conveys the perfect blend of business school wisdom with enlightened humour and playfulness. Your audience is guaranteed a high-octane, high-impact presentation, and the lessons last a lifetime.

> To have Steven Sonsino appear live at your next event
> email **booking@stevensonsino.com**
> or call us on +44(0)1234 252001

NOTES AND REFERENCES

1. Gookin, S. and D. (2002) *Parenting for Dummies* 2nd ed Wiley: A fabulously rich compendium of tools and tactics to help you lead two-year-olds or senior executives.

2. Goleman, Daniel (1998) *Working with Emotional Intelligence* Bloomsbury
Of Goleman's various books this is the most useful for pratising managers.

3. 1 Scott, C.R. et al.(1999) 'The impacts of communication and multiple identifications on intent to leave' *Management Communication Quarterly* 12 (3) 400-435
Craig Scott's research shows that folks on the receiving end of poor communication are much more likely to leave your company than to stay

4. Robert Kaplan and David Norton's *Balanced Scorecard* (HBS, 1996) reminds us that there is more to business than financial metrics. Perhaps the most useful aspect of the scorecard approach is to do with involving people in setting their own objectives and goals (See Chapter 3 on engagement for more.)

5. Friedman, W.A. (2006) 'Give me that old-time motivation' *Harvard Business Review* 84(7): In a fascinating note from the frontline of the sales industry, Walter Friedman reminds us of the power of explanations as a sales tool.

6. Bill Watkins, who is still CEO of Seagate Technology, was profiled in Erika Brown's 2006 feature 'Drive Fast, Drive Hard', an allusion to the Aston Martin roadster that gets Watkins from A to B at breakneck pace. Find the full article in *Forbes* Jan 9, 2006, volume 177, issue 1, p92.

7. Latham, G.P. (2004) 'The motivational benefits of goal setting' *Academy of Management Executive* (18) 4

8. Daniel Pink's fascinating book (2006, Cyan) offers strong evidence that right brain emotional/creative thinking will be valued as much as left-brain logical in the future.

9. Kevin Kennedy's clear thinking on emotional maturity is well worth reading in full if you can get it. The piece is 'Manager as motivator' from *Executive Excellence,* June 2001.

10. Enough is enough. Bob Sutton's exciting book, *The No Asshole Rule*, is getting a lot of attention from people who don't need persuading that it's time to act.

11. *Built to last* is a recent classic, a must read if you're serious about leading.

12. Robert Hurley's work on micromanagement shows decisively that high performing managers are their own worst enemies. Their burning drive to get things done and to succeed is matched only by their escalating fear of failure. The answer? Self belief and self confidence, says Hurley. 'Making the transition from micromanager to leader' (2006) by Robert Hurley and James Ryman is available online.

13. *Fast Company* pulls some brave features out of the bag from time to time including this August 2004 survey of 'jerk' bosses: 'Jerk bosses: to coach or can?'

14. Professor John Hunt's easy-to-read 1992 book *Managing people at work* (3rd edition) covers the inside and outside of the Work Interest Schedule. Also, visit **www.MTS360.com**, the home of the survey team.

15. Biotechnology giant Genentech was the Best Company to Work for in the US in 2006, according to *Fortune*, but was bumped to the number two one slot in 2007 by Google.

16 *Scientific American* Maja Storch writing in April 2005 crafted 'Make yourself happy'. Small acts that create immediate pleasures can add up to long-term satisfaction, she reports.

17. Geoffrey Colvin writes in *Fortune* in January 2006 that building a culture of trust is extremely difficult if not impossible. CEOs are more likely to have a single trusted advisor than to trust a group of senior executives.

18. Levin writes cogently on the subject of the return on investment of trust in *Corporate Construction Advisor* (2002).

19, 20. A great story, one of many on the subject, from the Associated Press newswire service in January 2006.

21. Richard Reeves 'The trouble with trust' *Management Today* Haymarket Business Publications March 2005 p33

22. Developing positive employee relations is no easy matter and requires a long-term perspective. But in the long run, the firms that stay the course and make the investment are not likely to regret it. Fulmer, I.S., Gerhart, B., & Scott, K.S. (2003) 'Are the 100 Best better? An empirical investigation of the relationship between being a "great place to work" and firm performance' *Personnel Psychology*, 56(4): 965–993.

23. Jean Hill speaks passionately about the balance between tight control and letting employees have the freedom to run their own lives in her interview with Cornell University's Department of Economics and Management (www.eclips.cornell.edu).

OTHER USEFUL READING

Branham, Leigh, (2005) *The 7 hidden reasons employees leave* Amacom

Bruch, H. and Ghoshal, S. (2005) *A bias for action* Harvard Business School Press

Buckingham, M. and Coffman, C. (1999) *First, break all the rules* Simon & Schuster

Bunting, Madeleine (2004) *Willing slaves: how the overwork culture is ruling our lives* Harper Perennial

Collins, Jim (2001) *Good to great* Random House Business Books

Corporate Research Foundation (2002) *The Best Companies to Work for in Australia* Allen & Unwin

Druskat, Vanessa, Mount, Gerald, and Sala, Fabio Editors (2005) *Linking EI and Performance at Work* Lawrence Erlbaum

Goleman, Daniel (1998) *Working with Emotional Intelligence* Bloomsbury

Kouses and Posner (1999) *Encouraging the heart* Jossey-Bass

Nicholson, Nigel (2003) 'How to motivate your problem people' in *Harvard Business Review*, January 2003, HBS Press

Pfeffer, Jeffrey (1998) *The Human Equation: building profits by putting people first* HBS Press

Pfeffer, J. and Sutton, R.I. (2004) *The Knowing-Doing Gap* HBS Press

Philips. R. (2003) *Stakeholder theory and organizational ethics* Berrett-Koehler

Porter, Bigley and Steers (2003) *Motivation and work behaviour* (7th ed.) Irwin McGraw Hill

Quirke, B. (2996) *Communicating Corporate Change* McGraw Hill

Sayles, L.R. and Smith, C.J. (2005) *The rise of the rogue executive* Pearson Prentice Hall

Schneider, B. Hanges, P.J., Smith, D.B. and Salvaggio, A.N. (2003) 'Which comes first: employee attitudes or organizational financial and market performance?' in *Journal of Applied Psychology* 88(5) 836-851

Schieman, S., Whitestone, Y. K. and Van Gundy, K. (2006) 'The Nature of Work and the Stress of Higher Status' in *Journal of Health and Social Behaviour* (16) 242-257

Sirota, D., Mischkind, L.A. and Meltzer, M.I. (2005) *The enthusiastic employee: how companies profit by giving employees what they want* Wharton School Publishing

INDEX

ABOUT THE AUTHORS

Jacqueline Moore and Steven Sonsino are a husband and wife team who were originally involved in training media professionals before moving into the field of leadership development. 'The Seven Failings of Really Useless Leaders' is the third book they have written together

JACQUELINE MOORE is a business author and writer and her last book, *Leadership Unplugged*, was described as 'learned yet practical' by Harvard Business School Press. Until she turned to writing full-time in 2003, Jacqueline was a senior journalist on the London *Financial Times* where she worked for 16 years. She worked on the News and Features desks of the *Financial Times* as well as on the World Stock Markets page. She was launch production editor of the Business Travel Page, launch writer and editor of the FT View column and launch editor and writer of the back page e-business column. In addition, she co-designed and co-taught the first Workshop & Facilitation Skills course on the MBA programme at Cranfield School of Management in the UK and is a former Director of the award-winning Journalism Training Centre.

STEVEN SONSINO is an author, motivational speaker and business school professor with clients including Microsoft, Sony Ericsson, Sara Lee, General Mills, E.On, the Institute of Chartered Accountants and the Chartered Institute of Personnel and Development. He is a Fellow of the Centre for Management

Development at London Business School where his recent clients include HSBC and ExxonMobil.

From 2001 until 2004 Steven was Director of the School's Emerging Leaders Programme and he founded the Tomorrow's Leaders Research Group at the School in 2002.

From 2002 until 2006 he directed The Leadership Alliance, a consortium programme run by London Business School with the Universities of Lisbon and Porto.

Steven is visiting professor at Escola de Gestão do Porto in Portugal, teaching leadership and negotiations. He is also a visiting professor at the European School of Management and Technology in Berlin, teaching leadership. He recently became a visiting professor at the Indian School of Business, where he also teaches leadership.

Before beginning his doctoral research at the London School of Economics, Steven was founder and managing director of the award-winning Journalism Training Centre and previously he was Head of Editorial Training at the business publishing arm of Reed-Elsevier, the Anglo-Dutch media company.

Before turning to leadership development, he was an Editor and journalist for publications including the *Financial Times*, *New Scientist*, *The Guardian* and *The Independent*, as well as making broadcasts for the BBC.

Steven broadcasts a video podcast on leadership style at **www.leadership.fm**.